THE TATTOO
Coloring Book

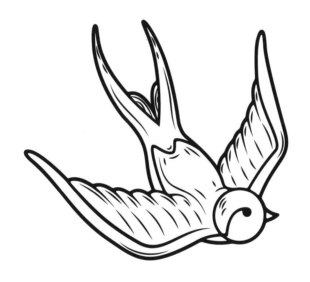

THE TATTOO Coloring Book

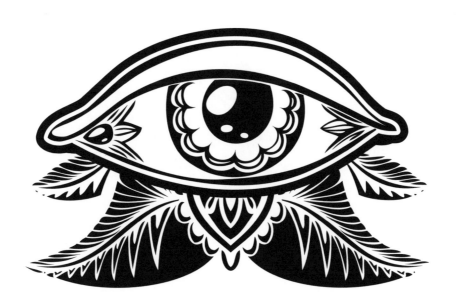

SIRIUS

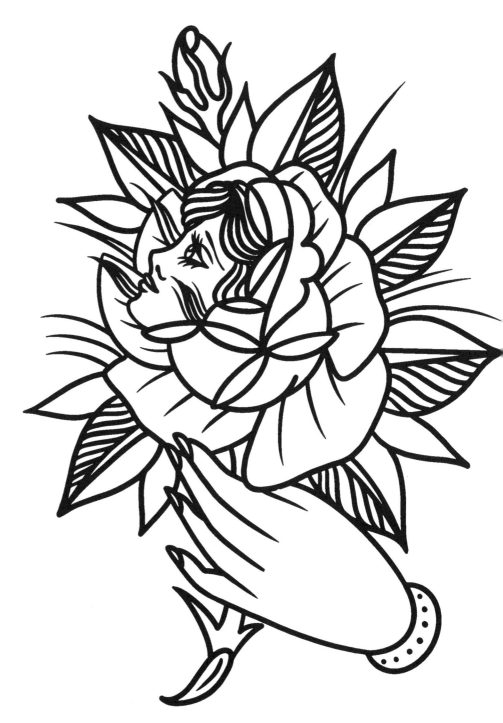

SIRIUS

This edition published in 2024 by Sirius Publishing, a division of
Arcturus Publishing Limited,
26/27 Bickels Yard, 151–153 Bermondsey Street,
London SE1 3HA

ISBN: 978-1-3988-4478-0
CH012192NT
Supplier 29, Date 0724, Print run 6646

Printed in China

INTRODUCTION

Humans have been creating permanent designs on their bodies for more than 5,000 years. Tattoos have been signifiers of status, rites of passage, and achievement for many different peoples all over the world The word comes from the Samoan tatau which means "to strike." In western societies, the status of tattoos has undergone quite a revolution over the past 20–30 years. Once the preserve of sailors—who marked their travels with a tattoo—and prisoners, they are now found on people in all walks of life. Some are still used to show membership of a group, but many are simply a form of artistic expression. This selection of tattoos includes traditional maritime symbols, but also more modern interpretations. All are graphically interesting and fascinating to color. You just need to choose a favorite.

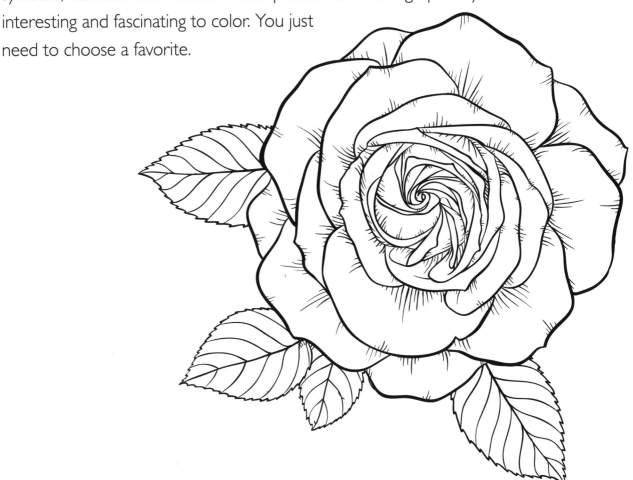

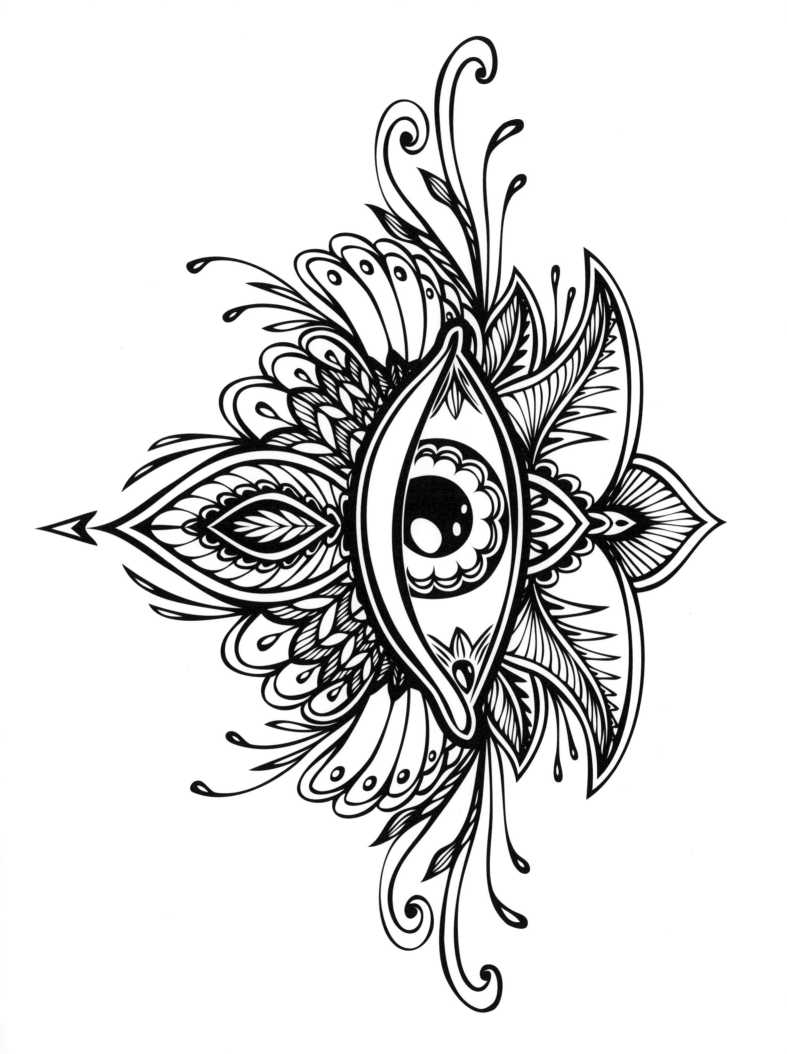

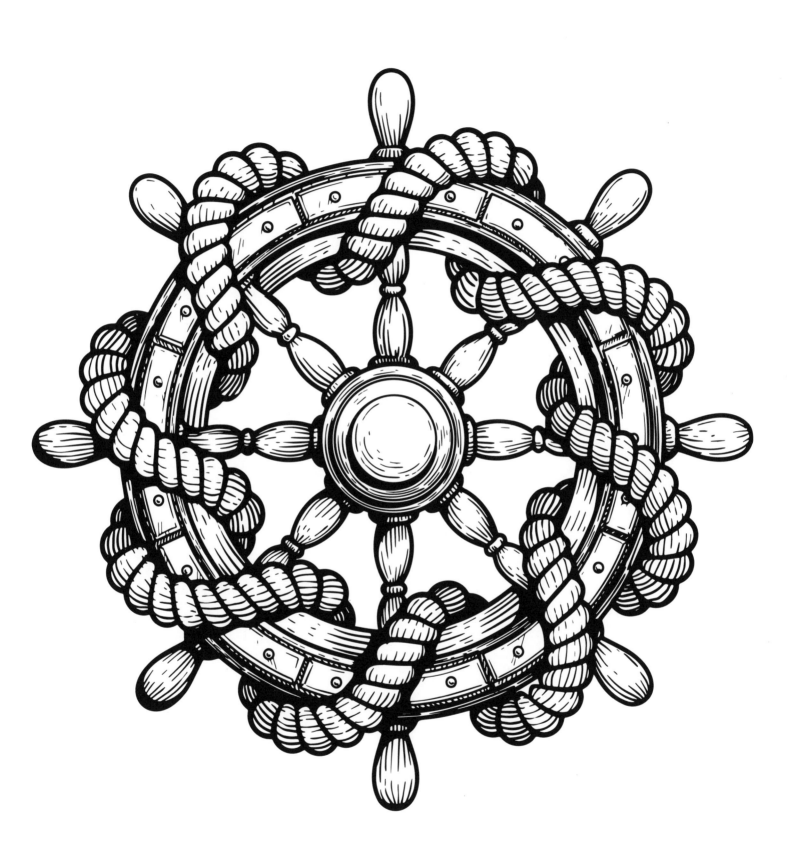

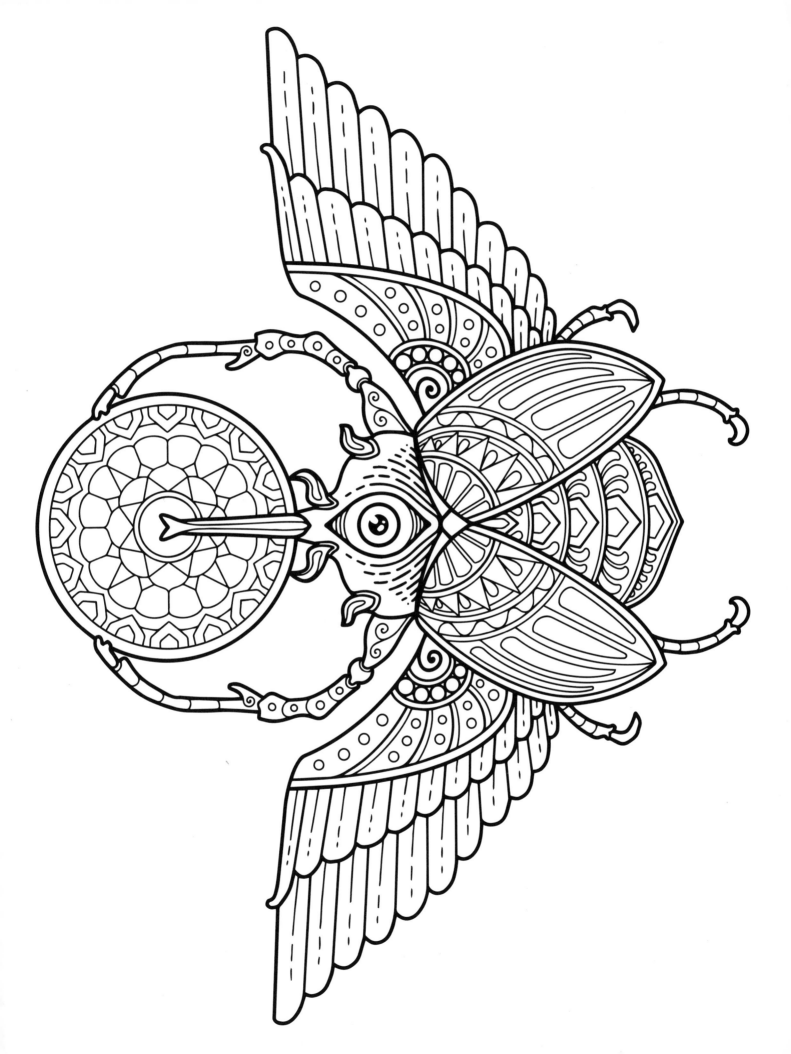

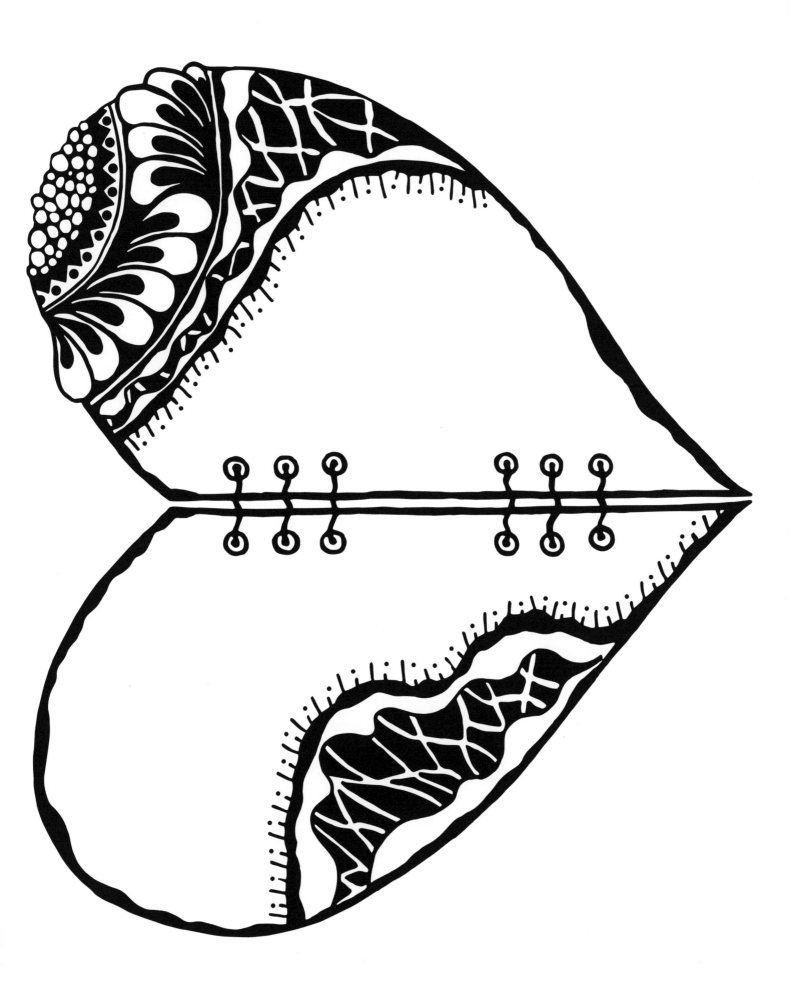

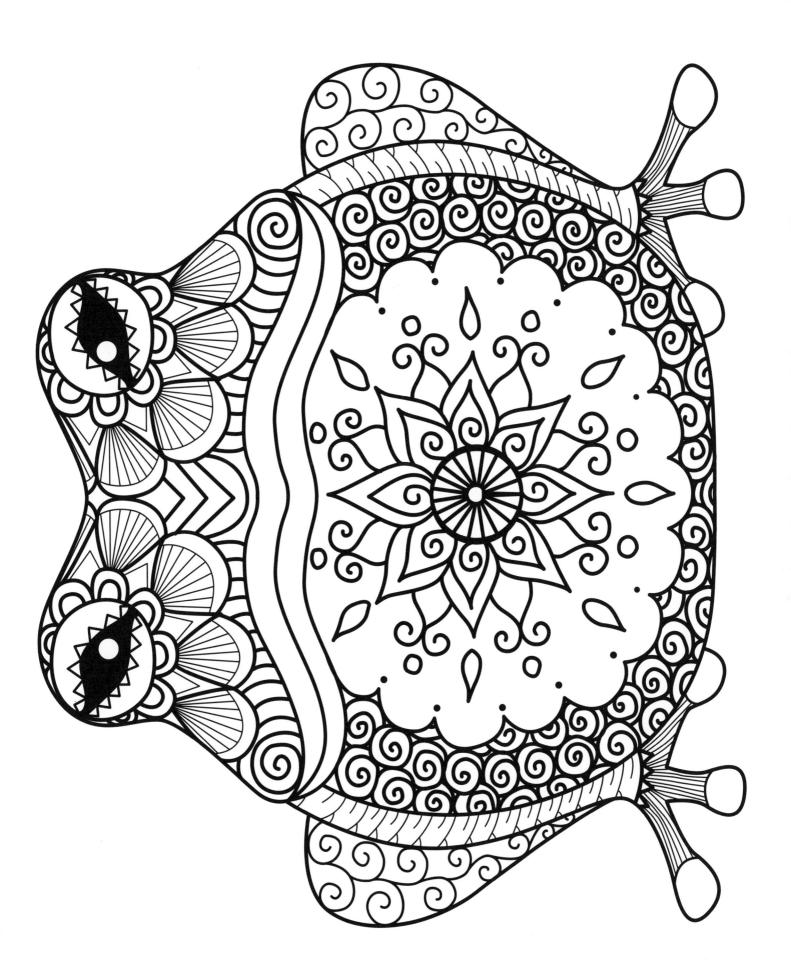

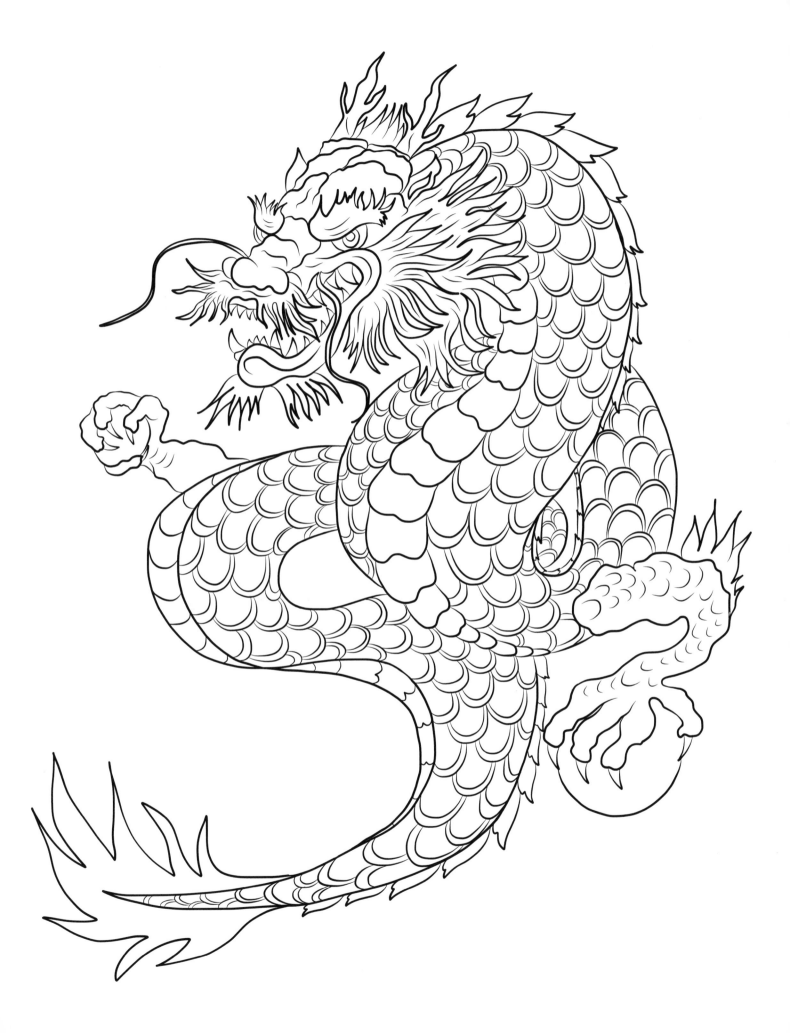

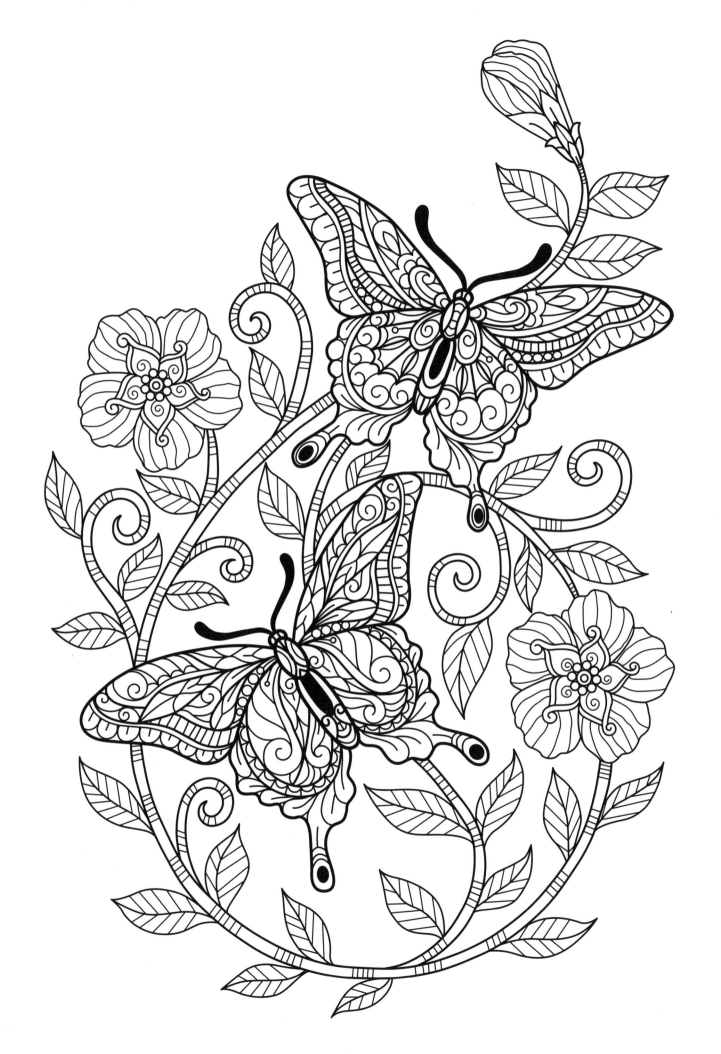

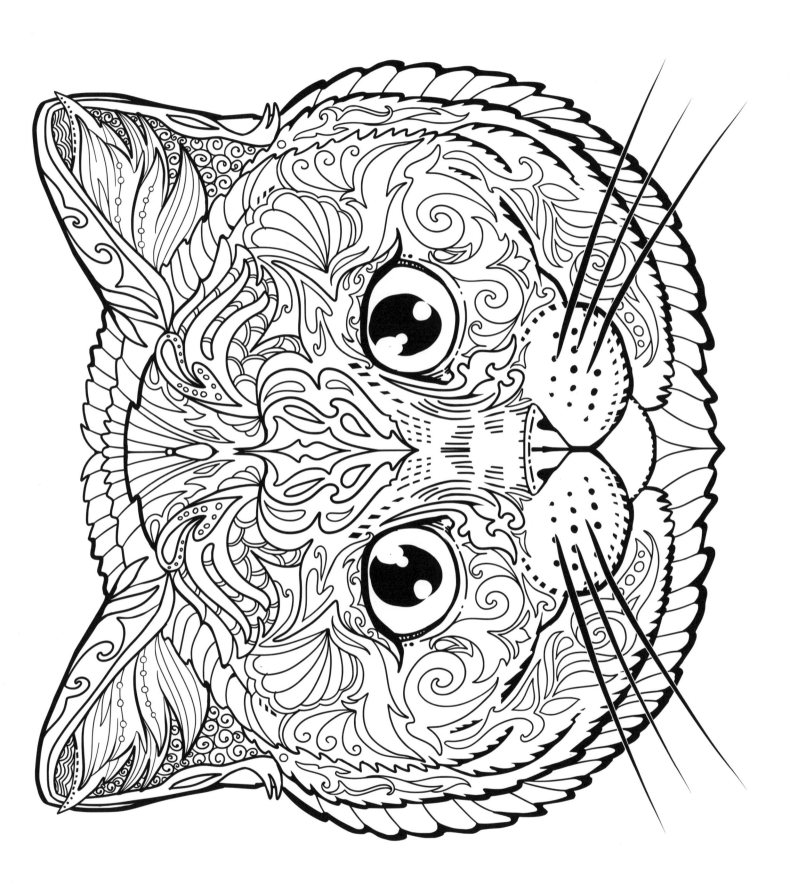

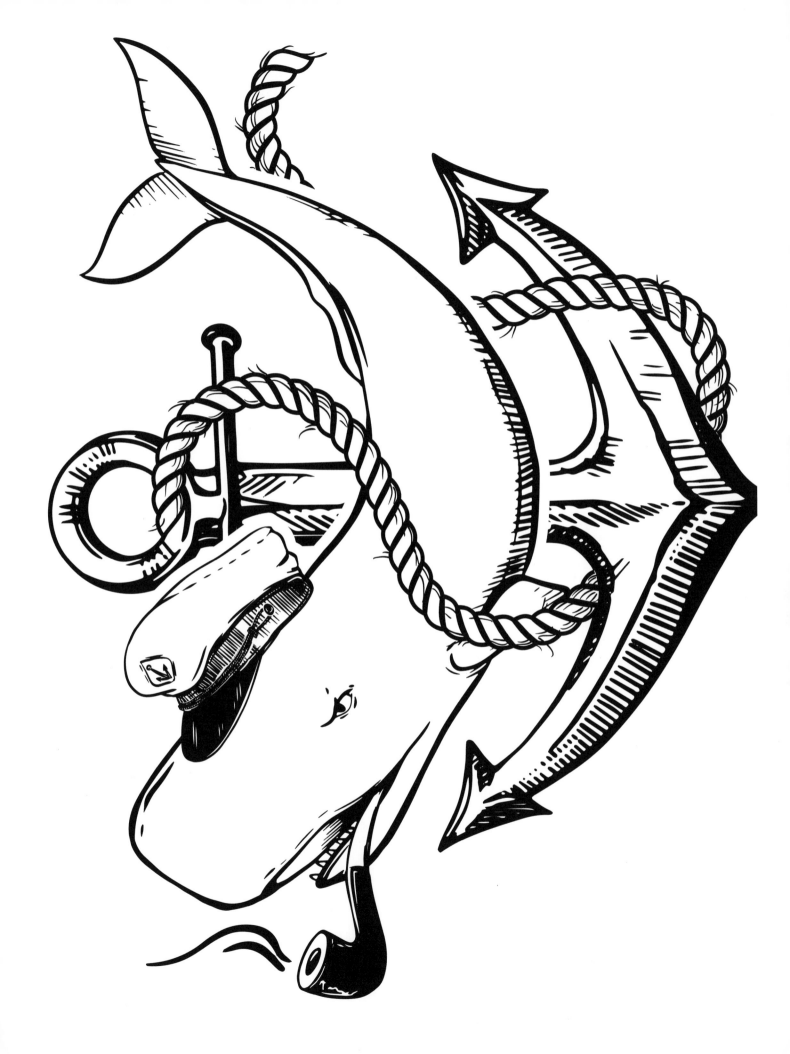

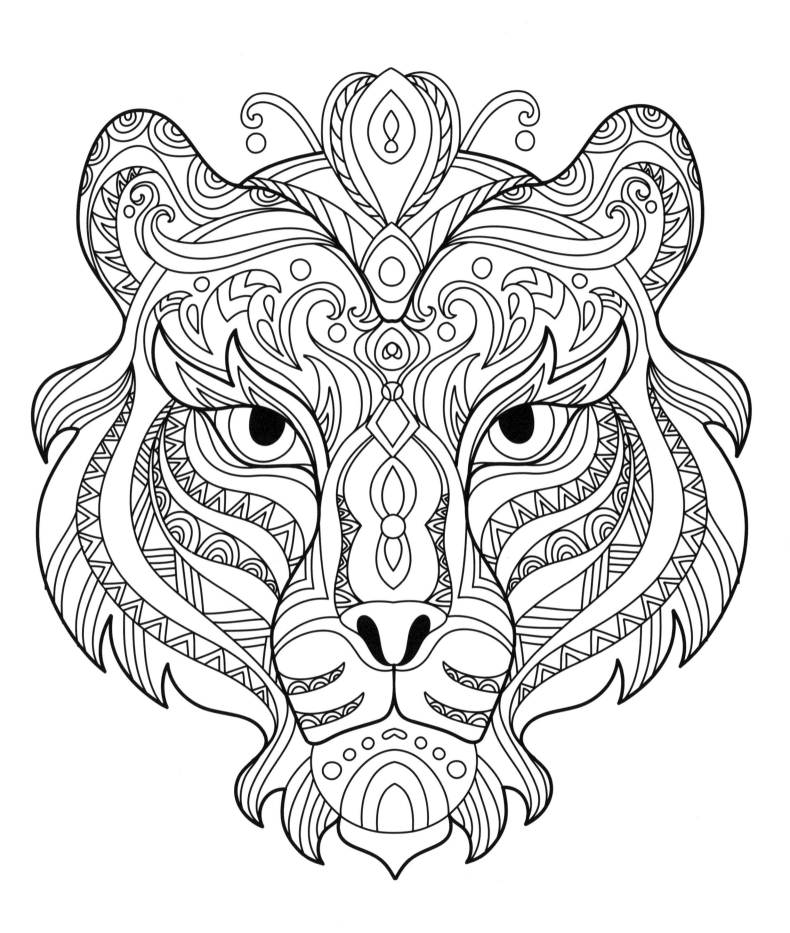

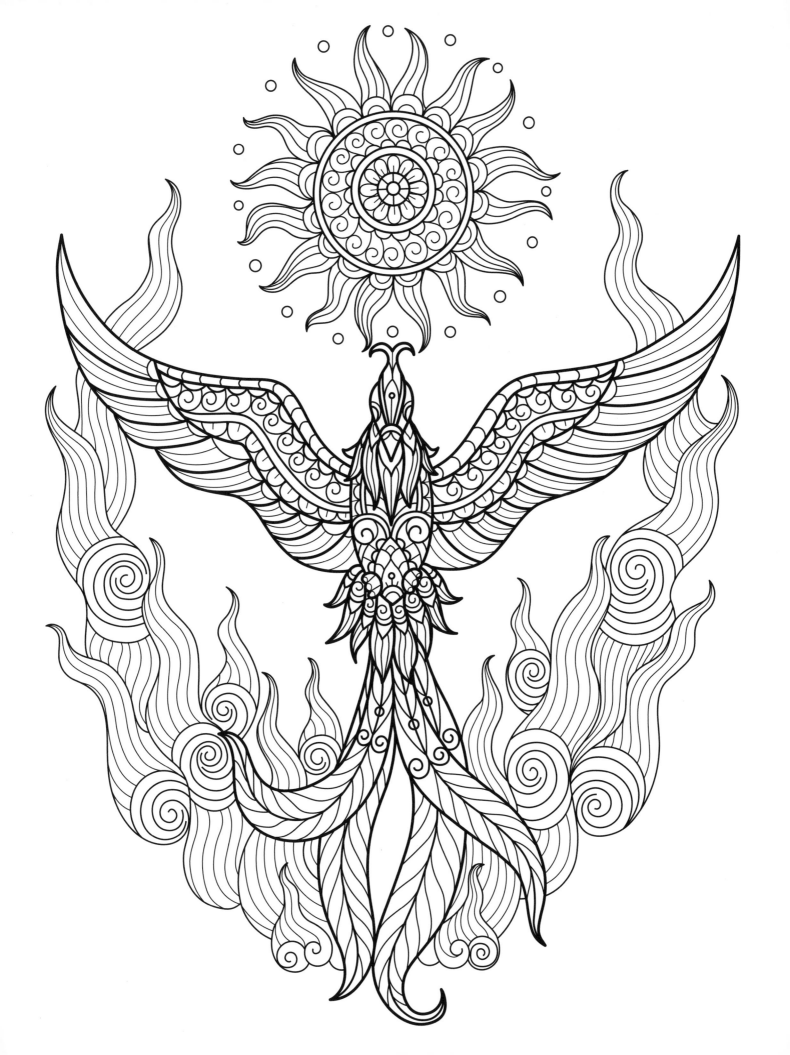

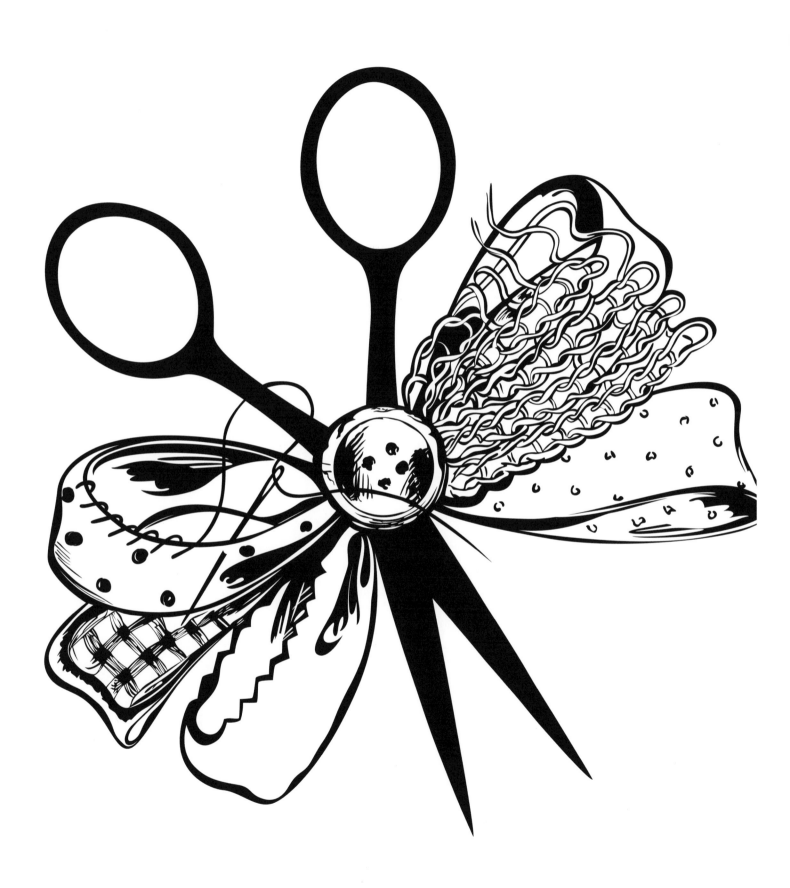

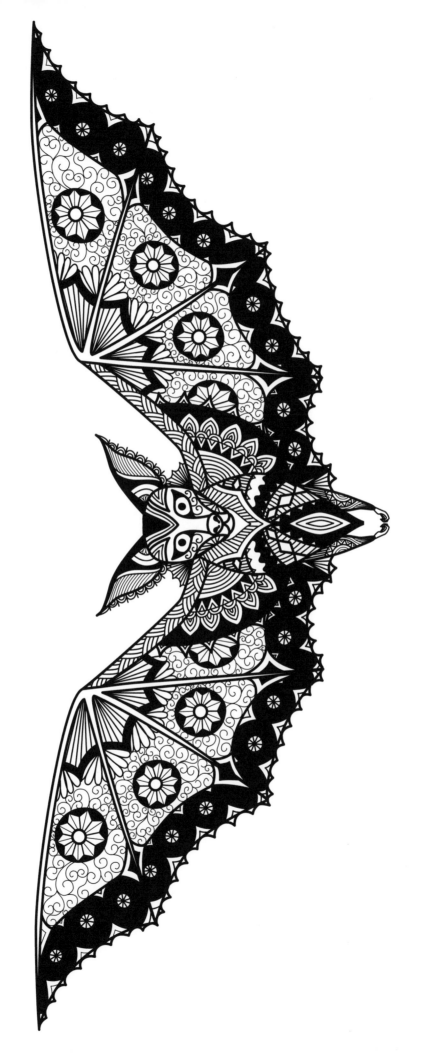

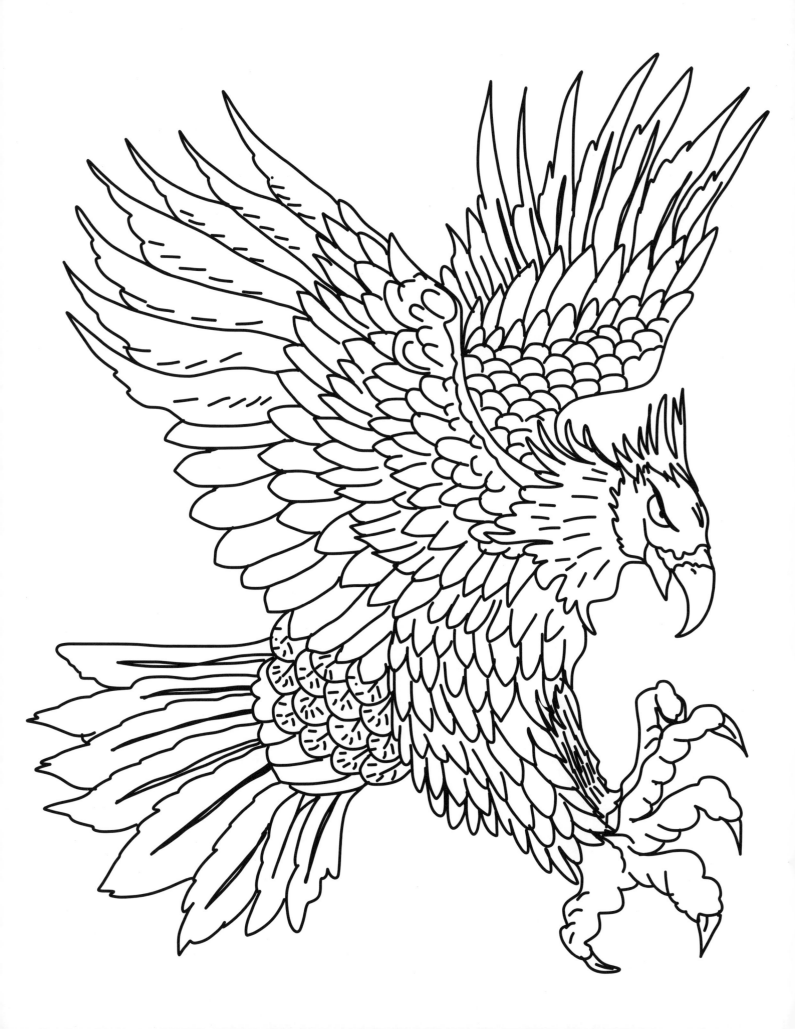

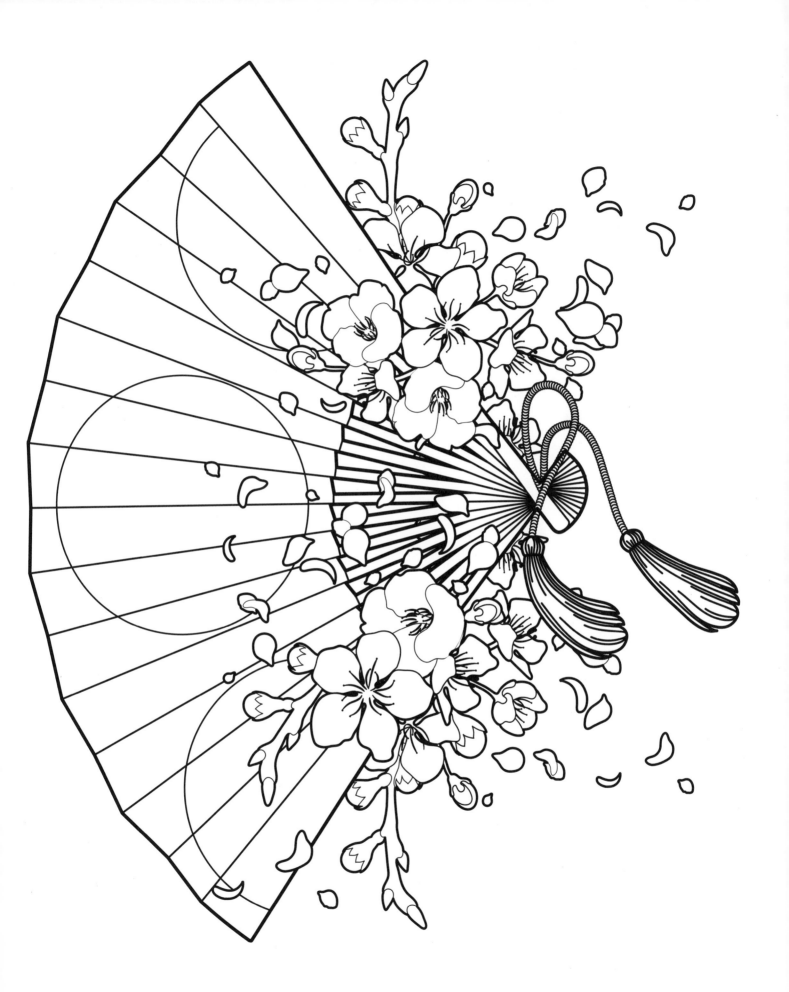

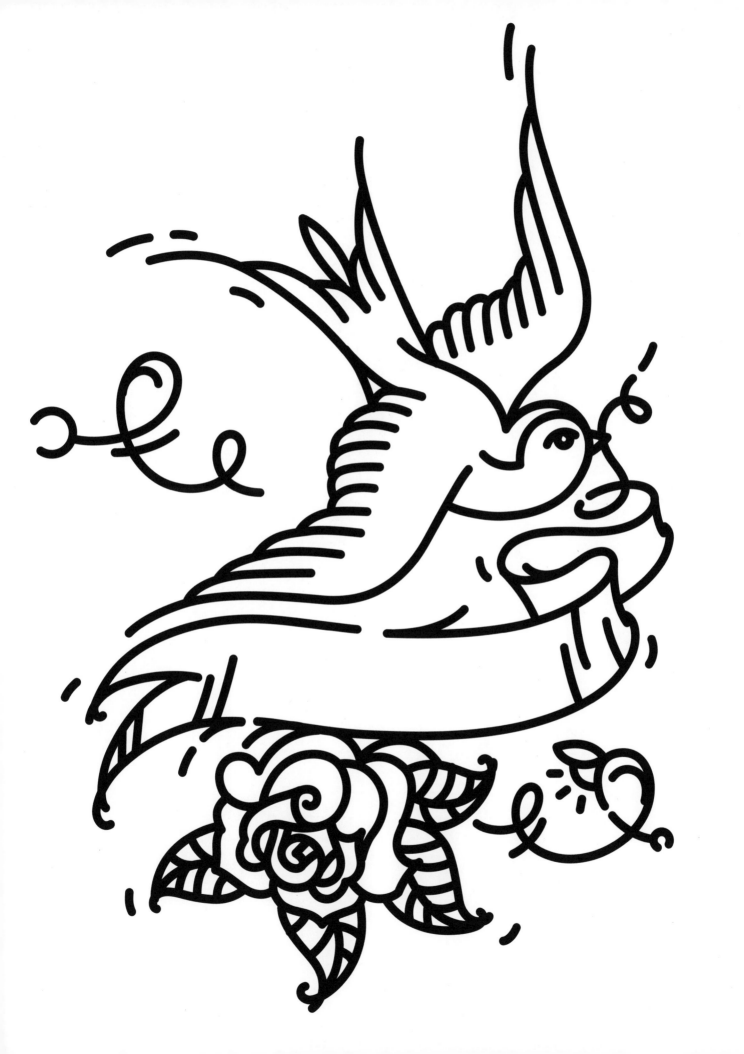

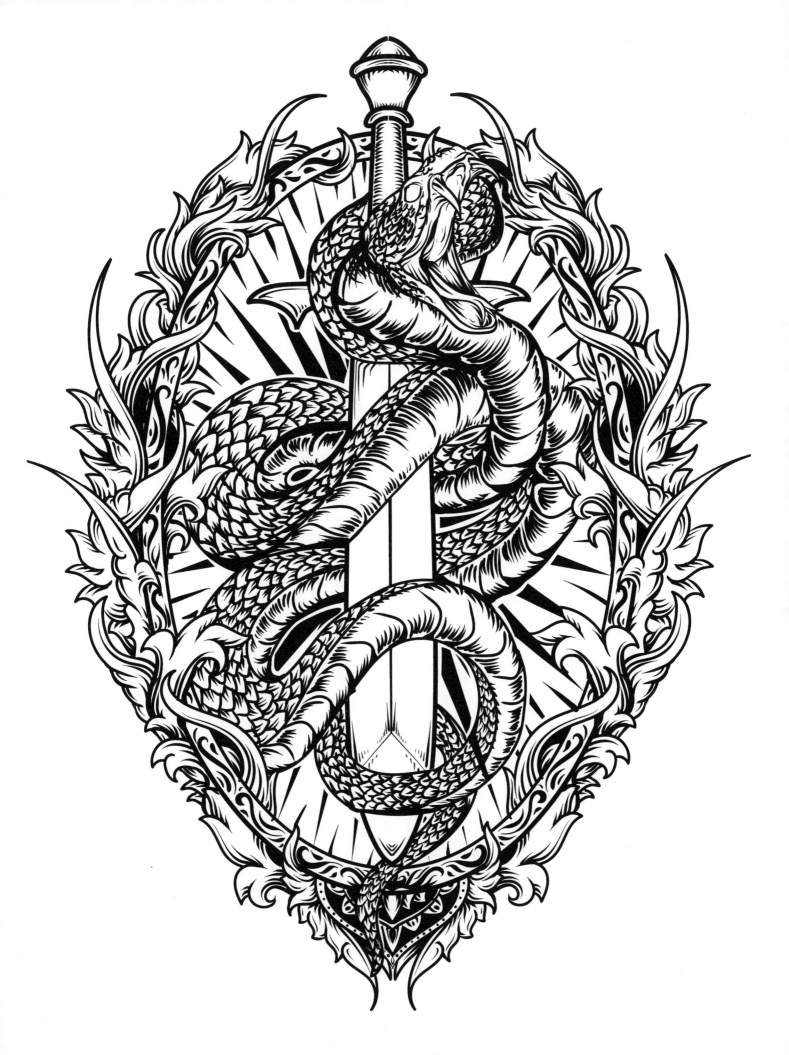

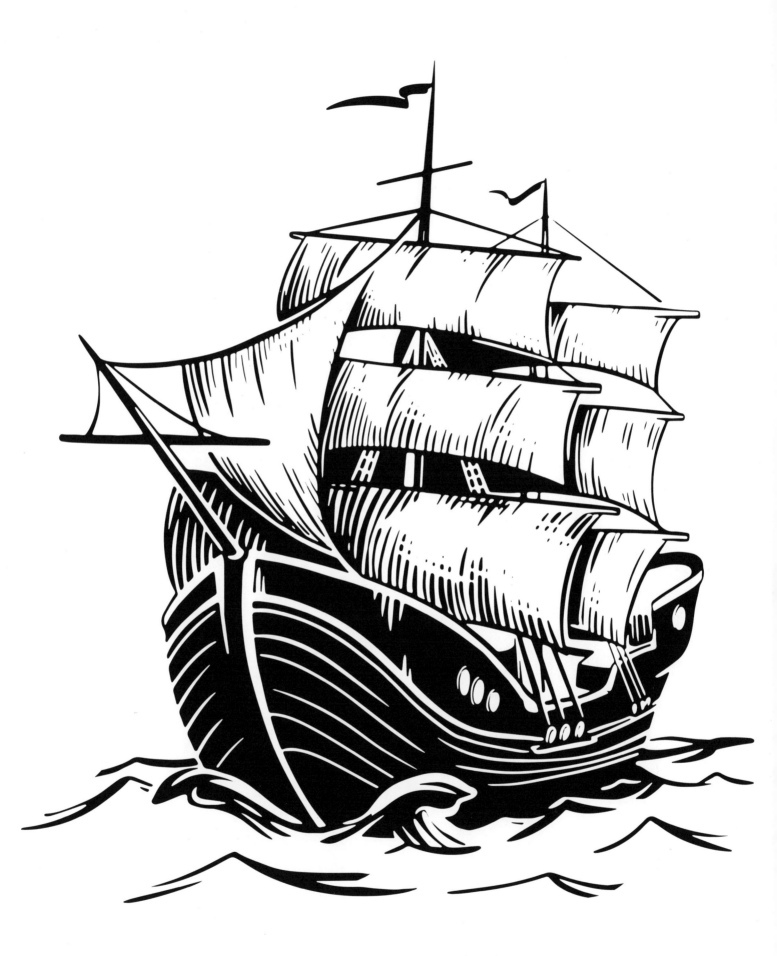

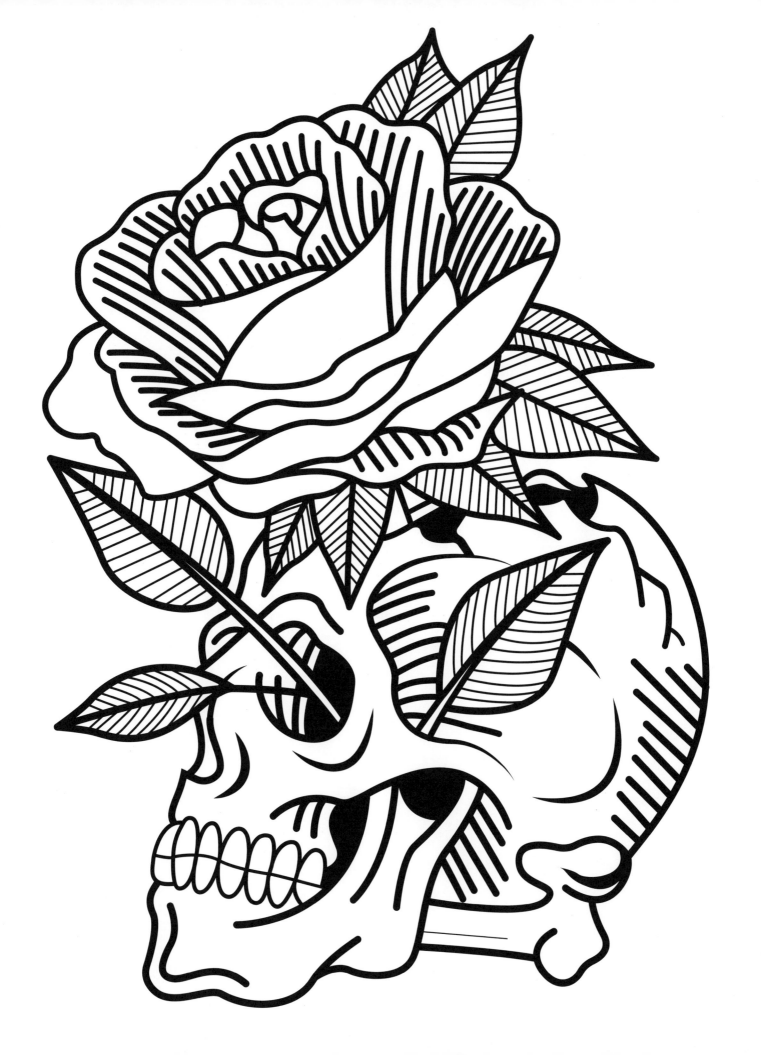

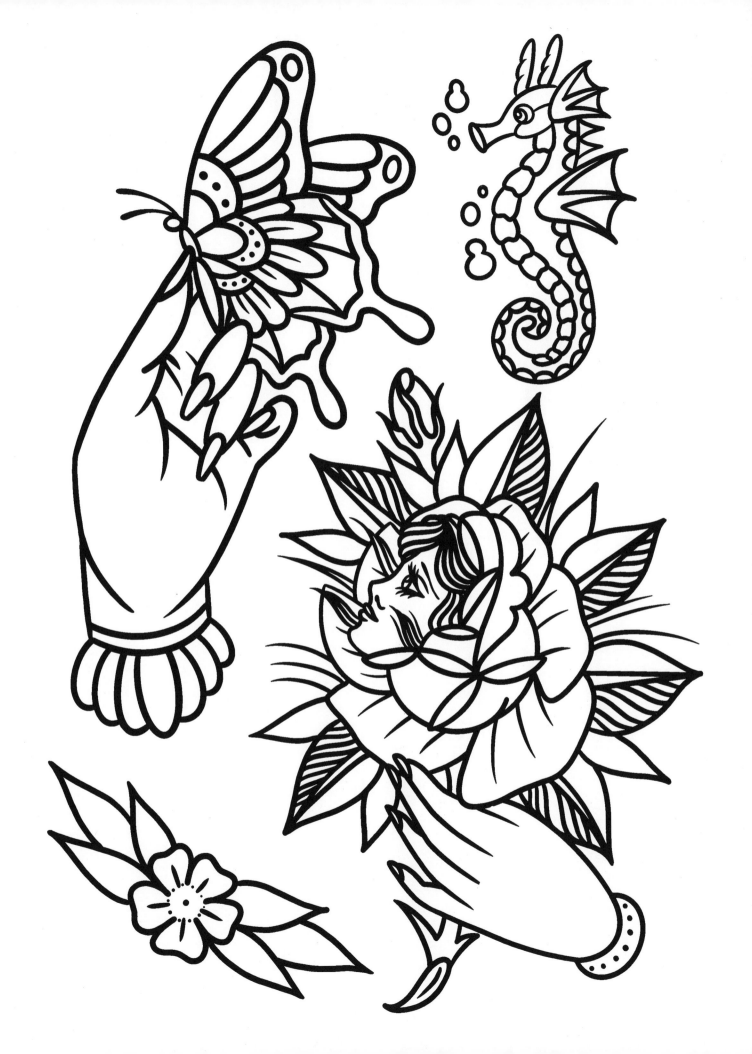

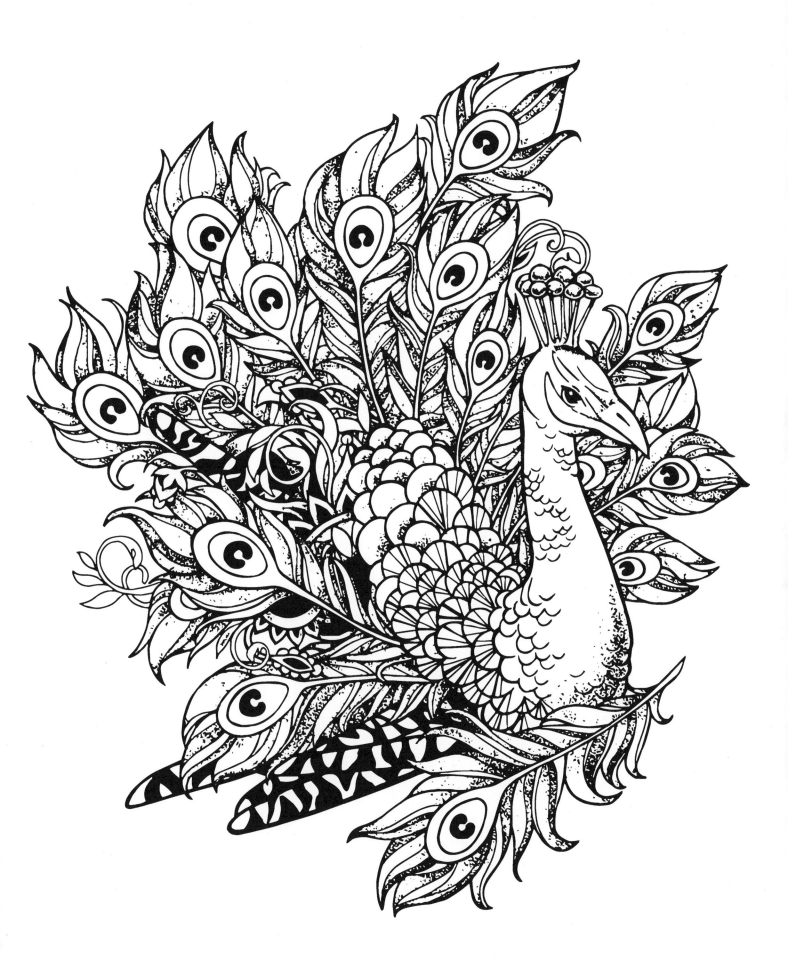

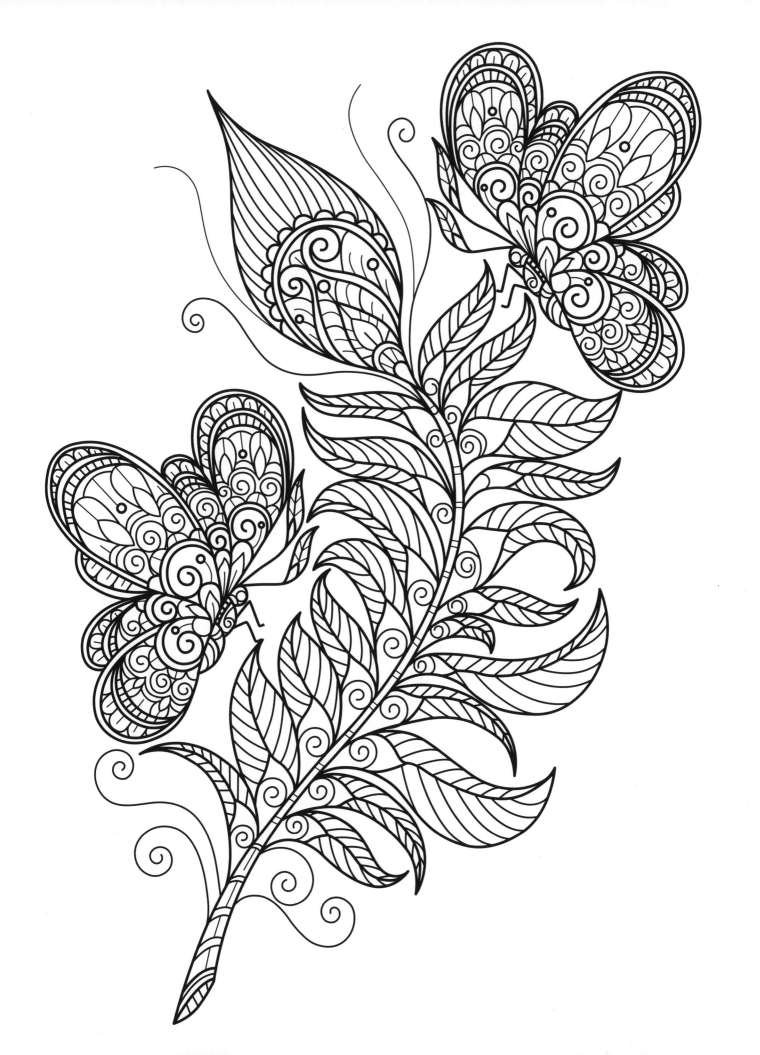

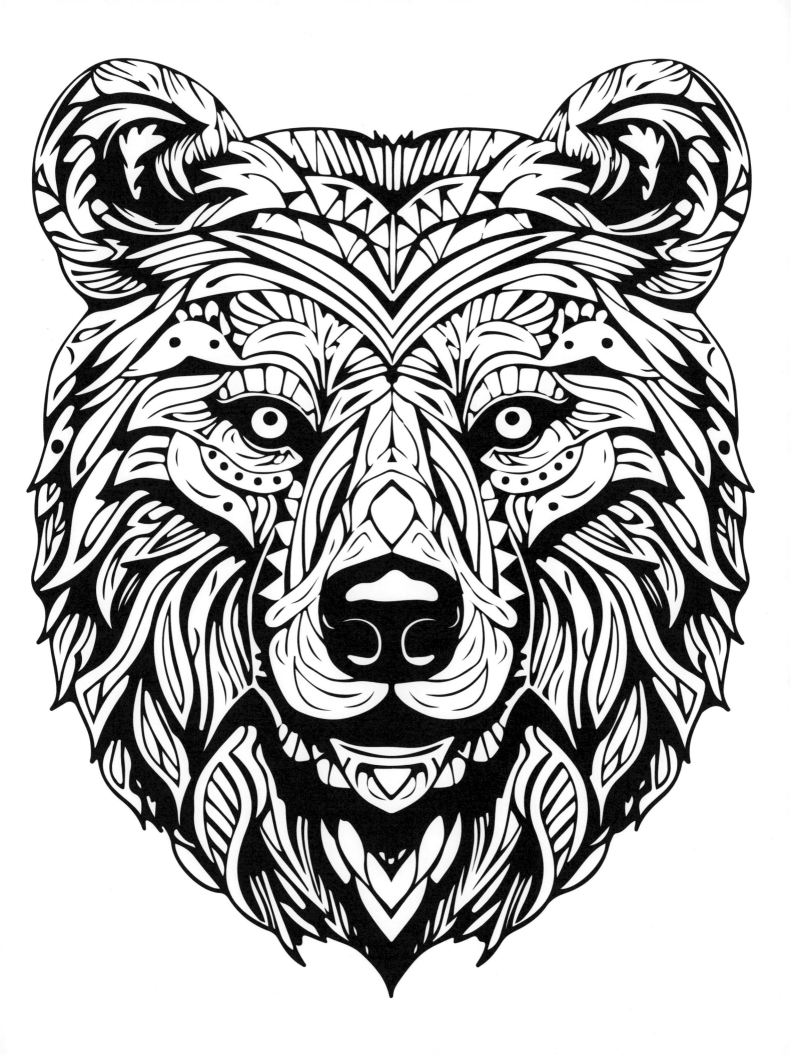

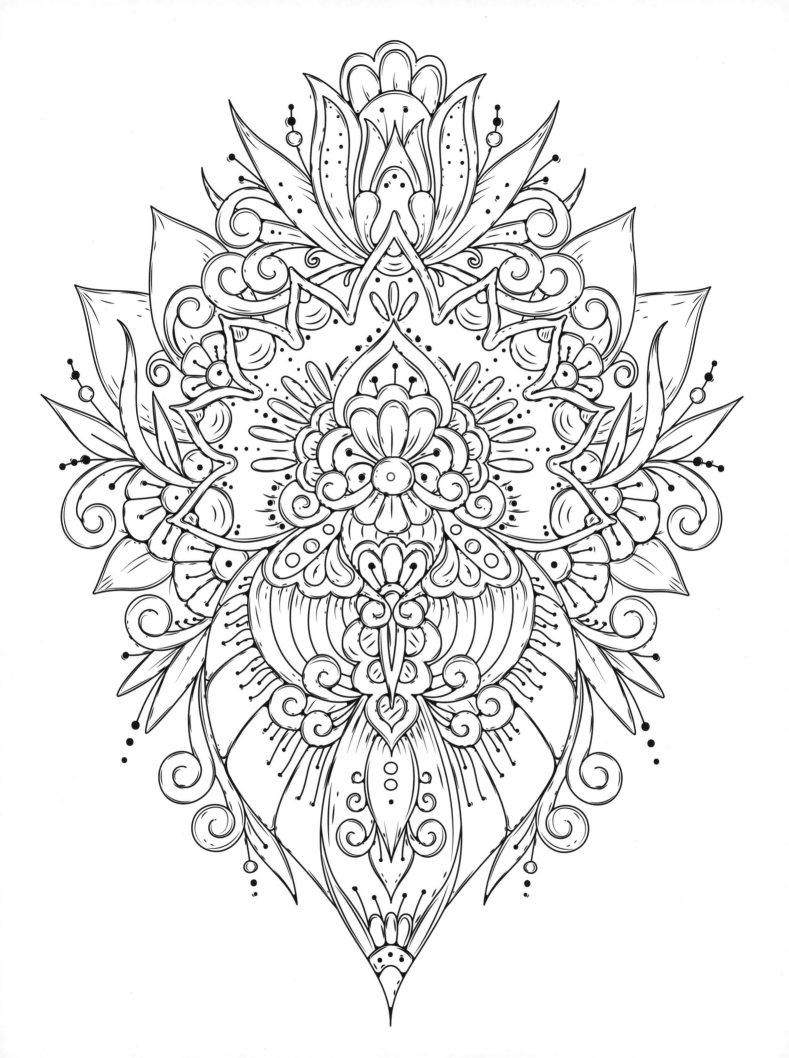

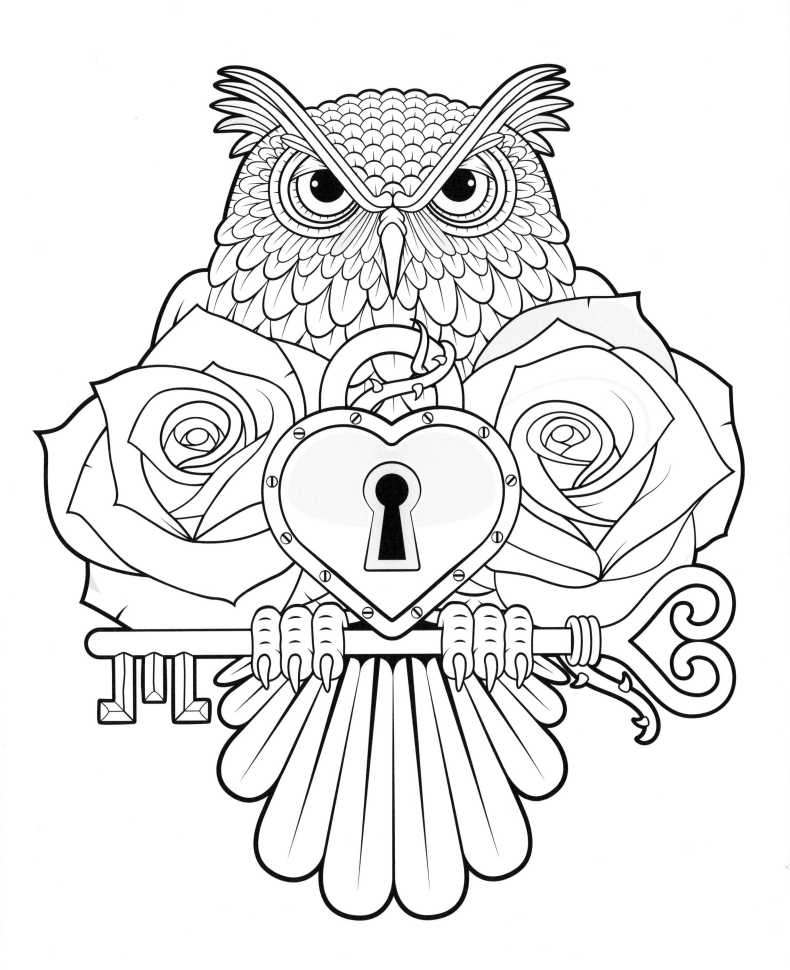

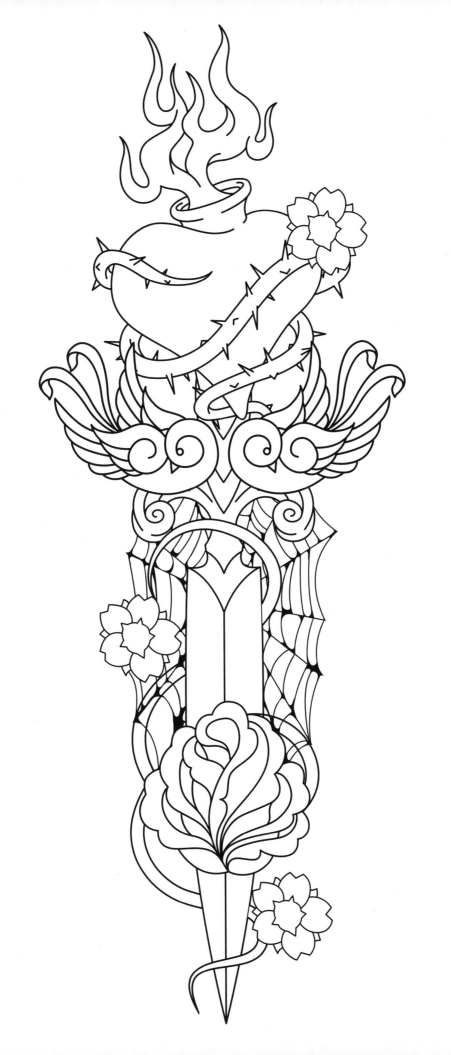

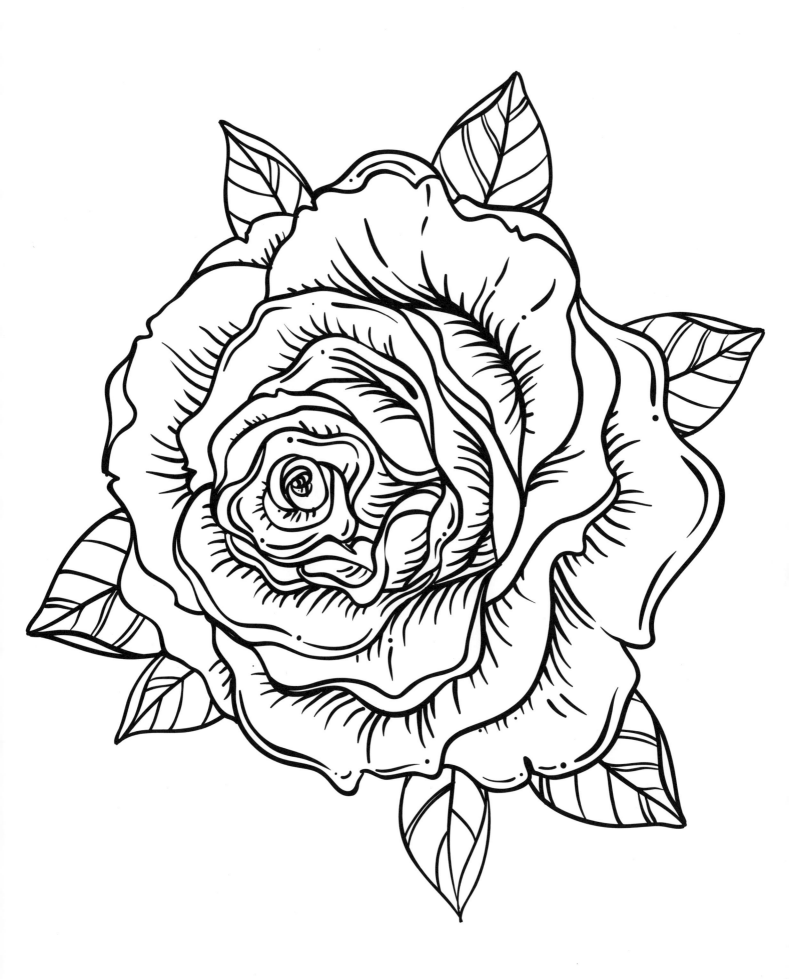

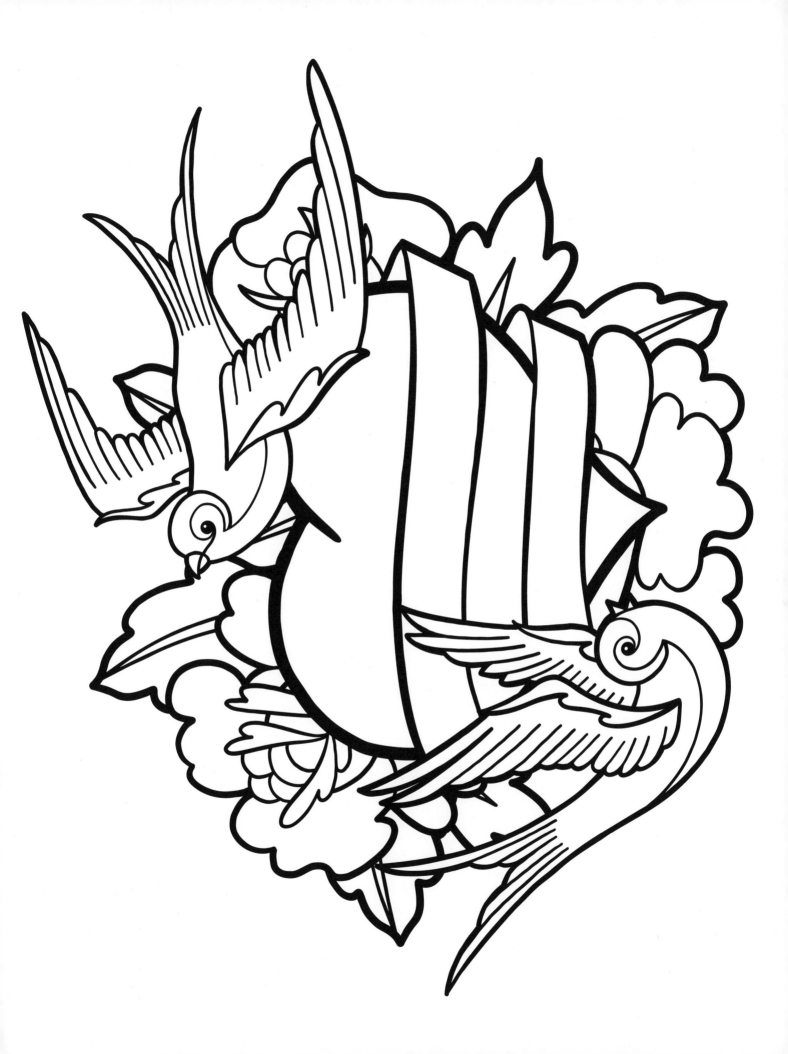

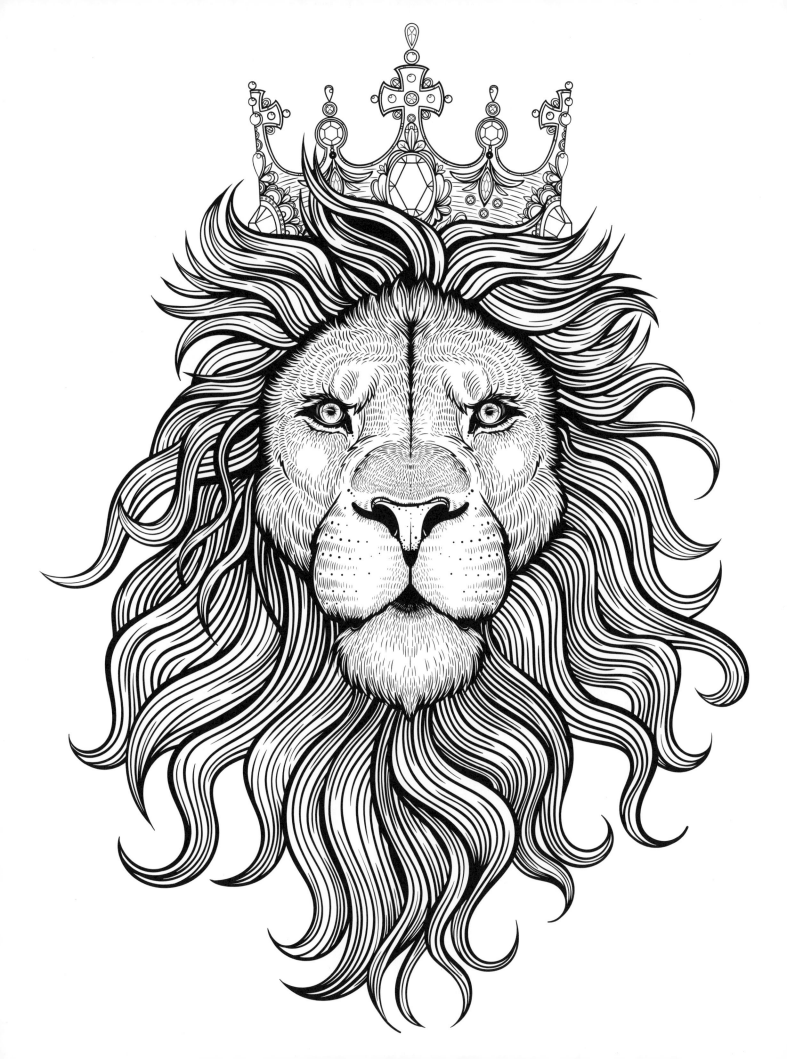

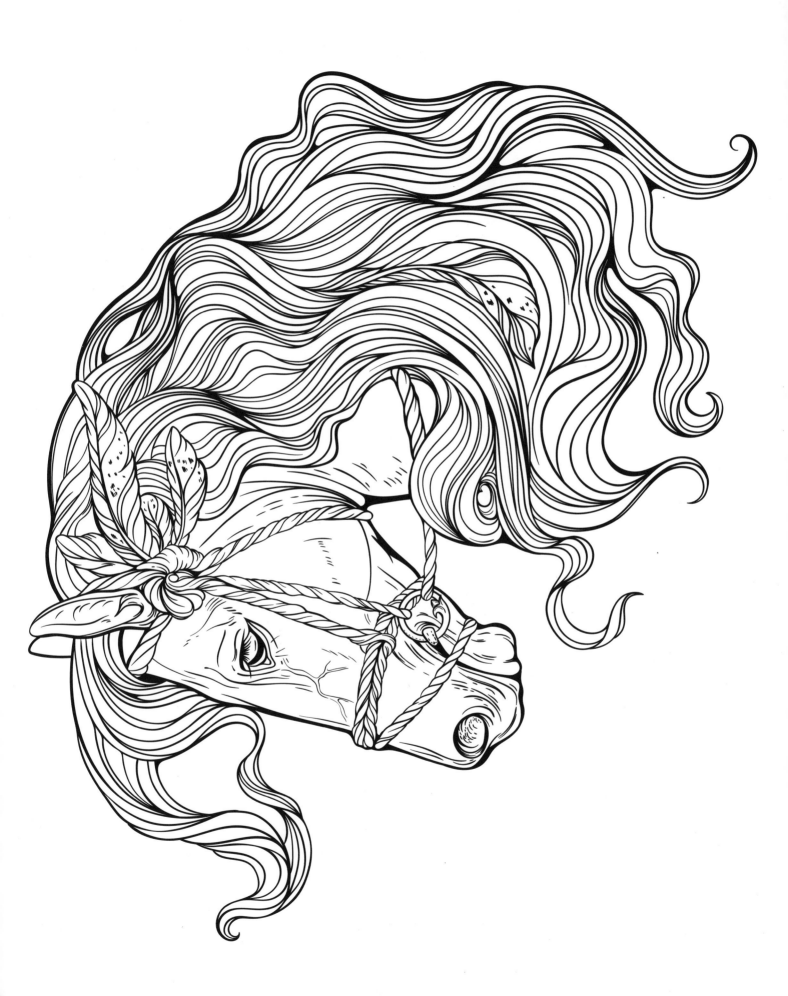

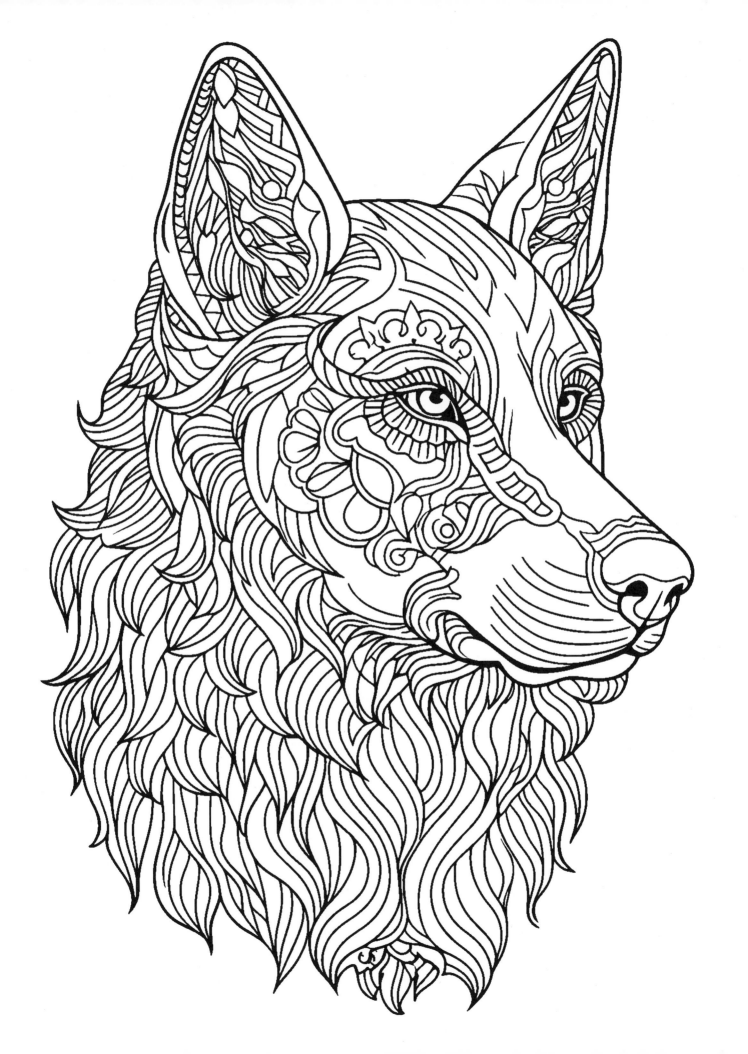

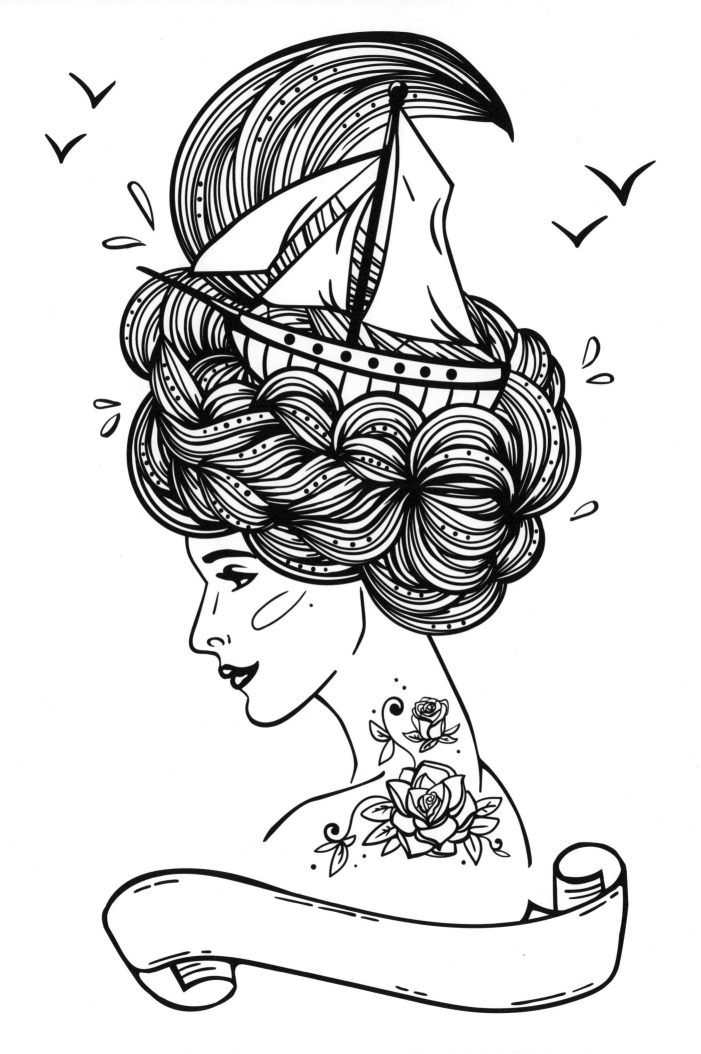

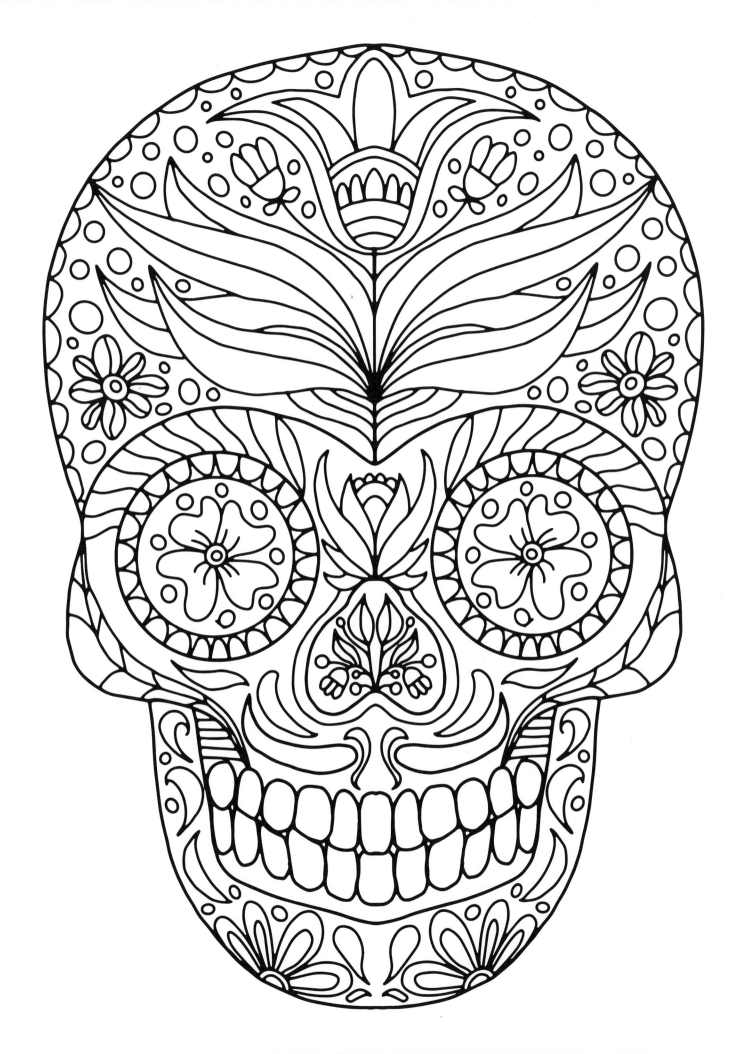

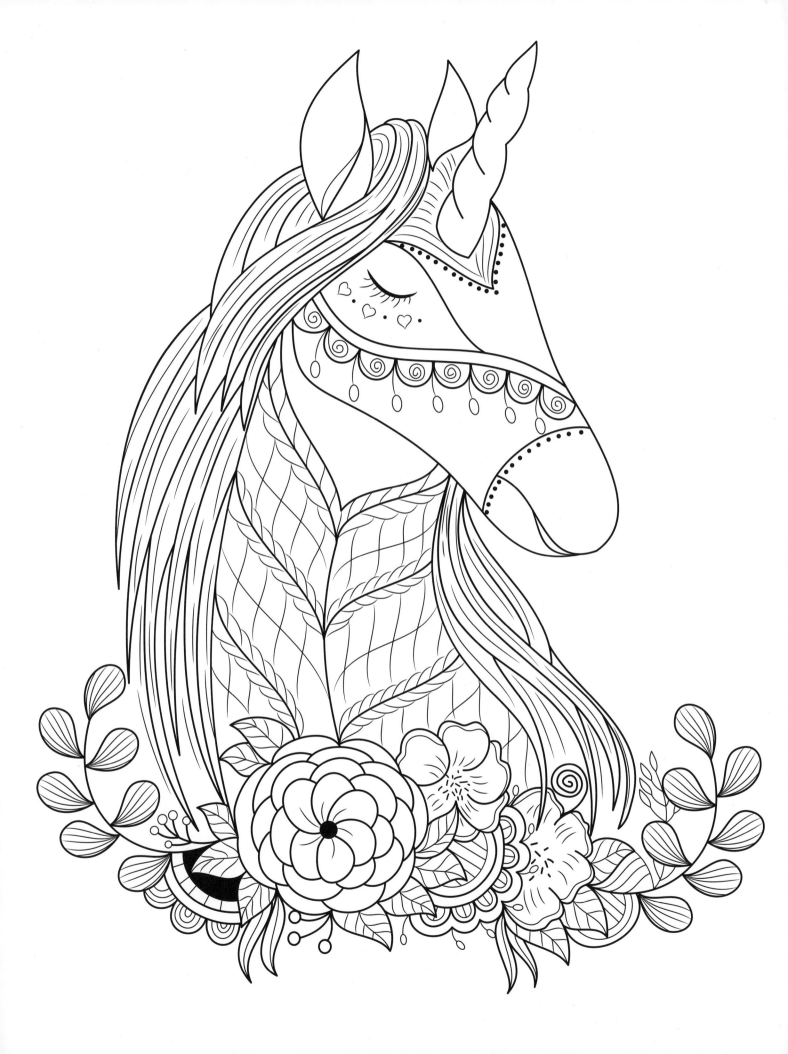

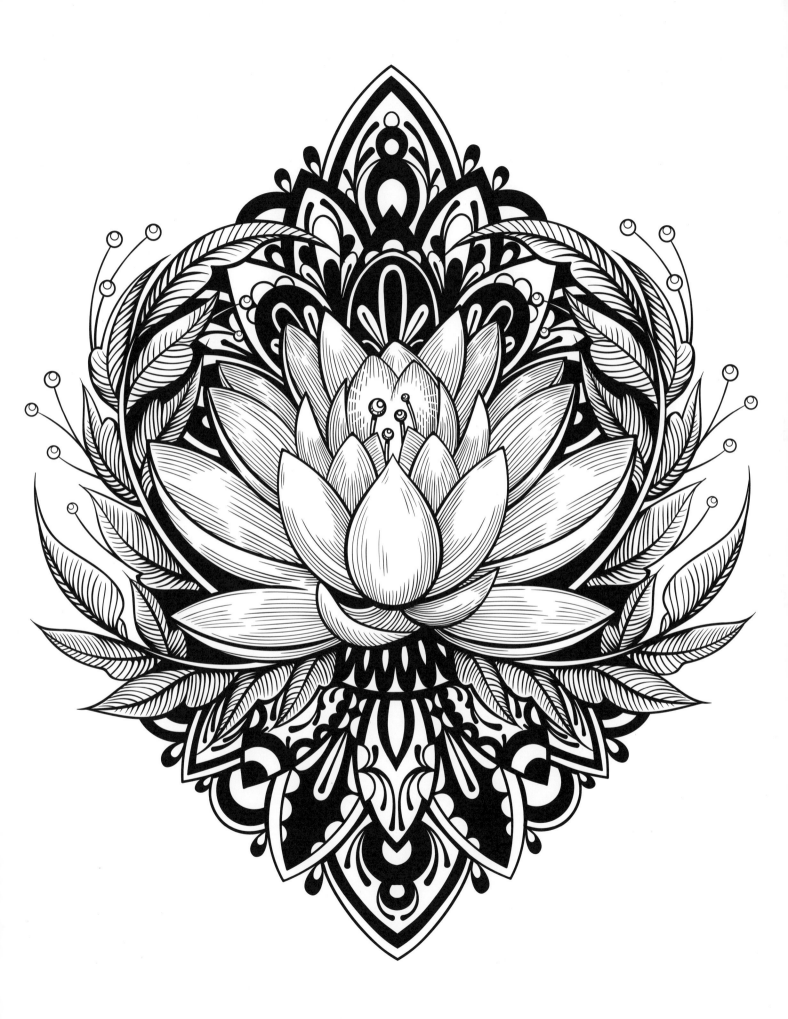

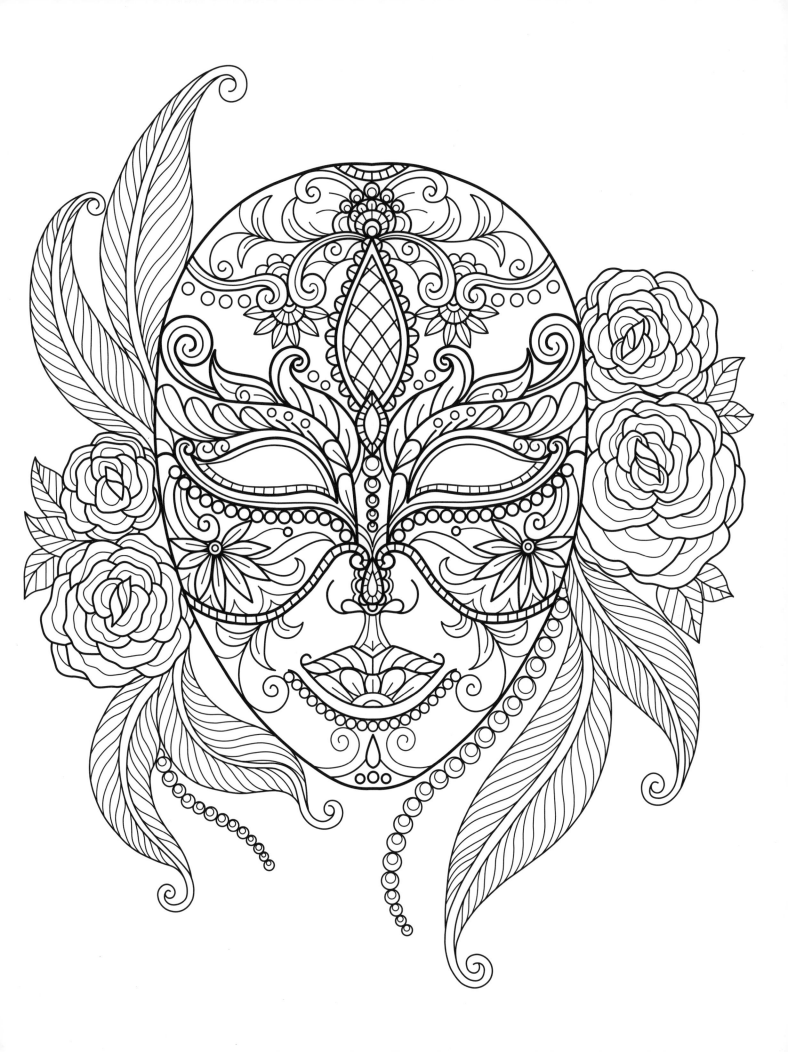

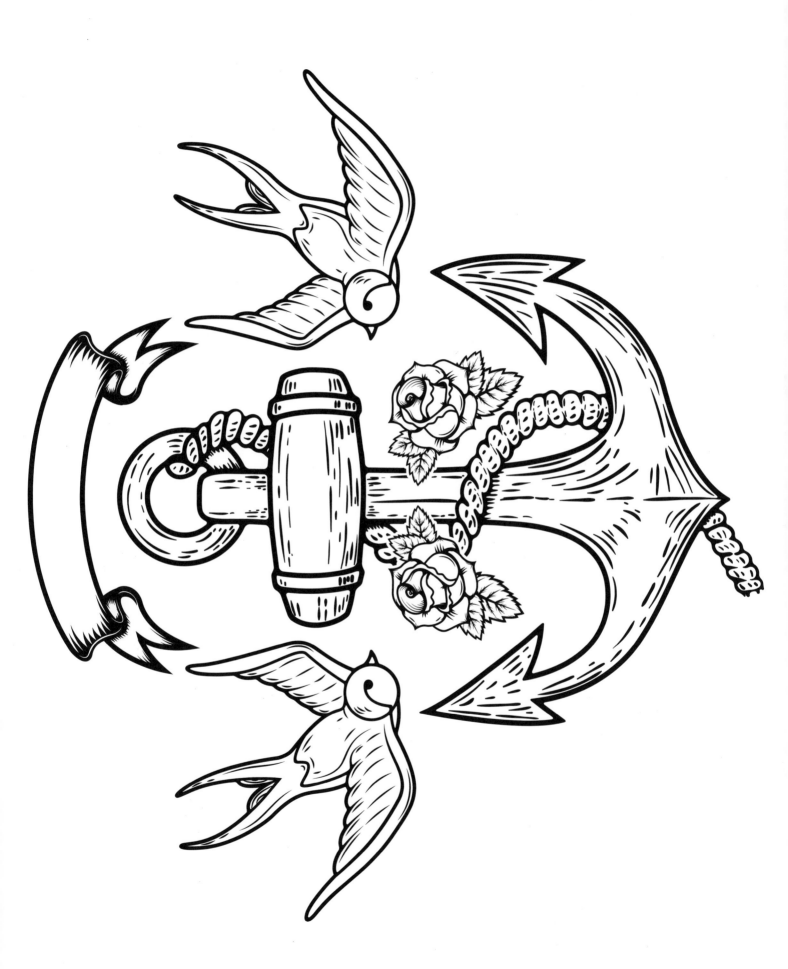

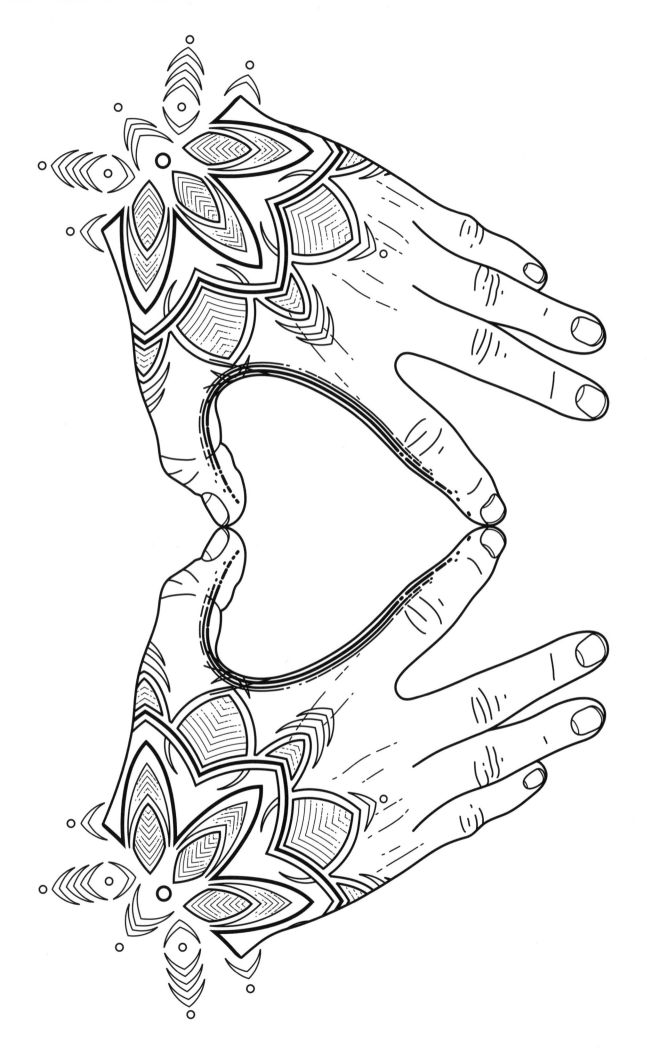

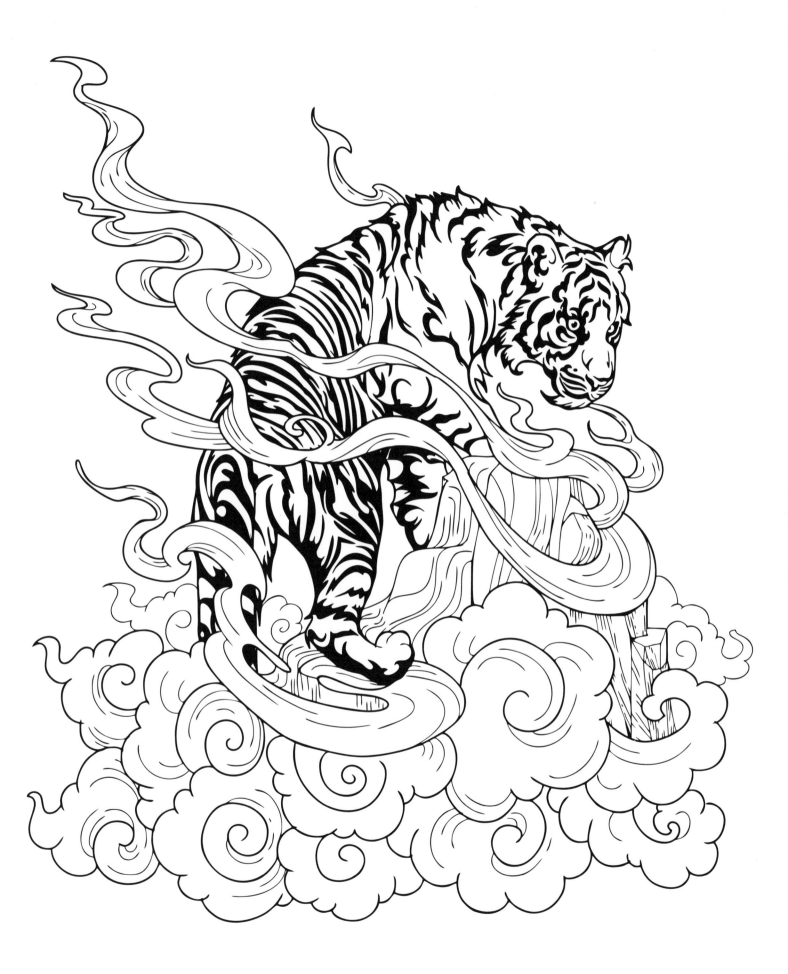

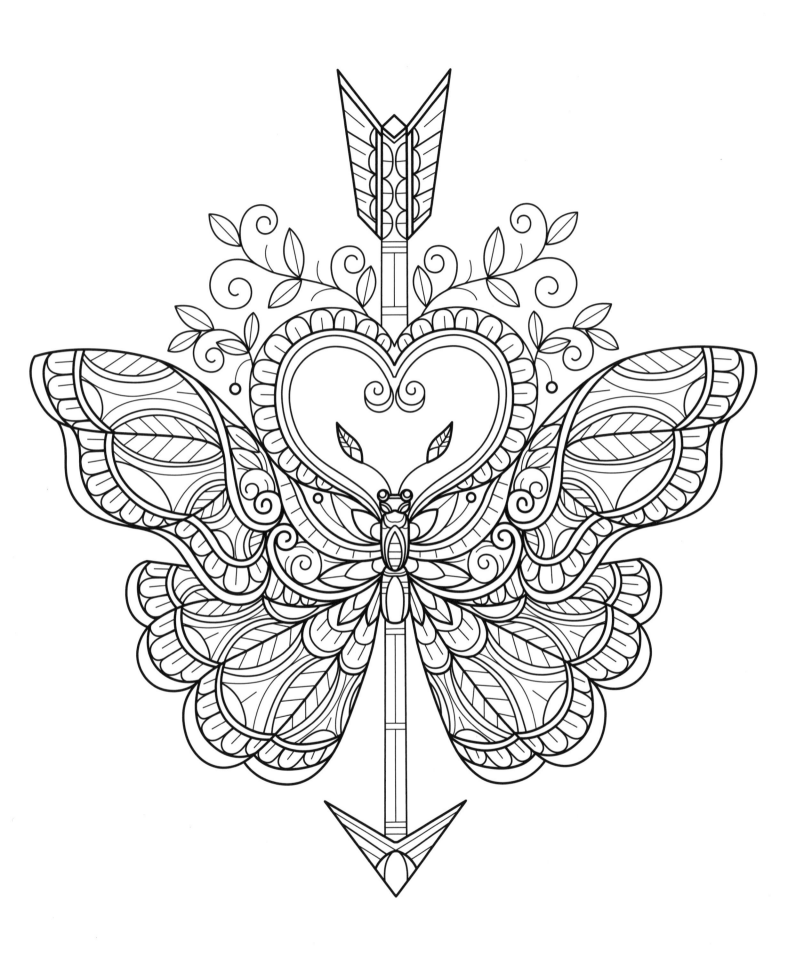

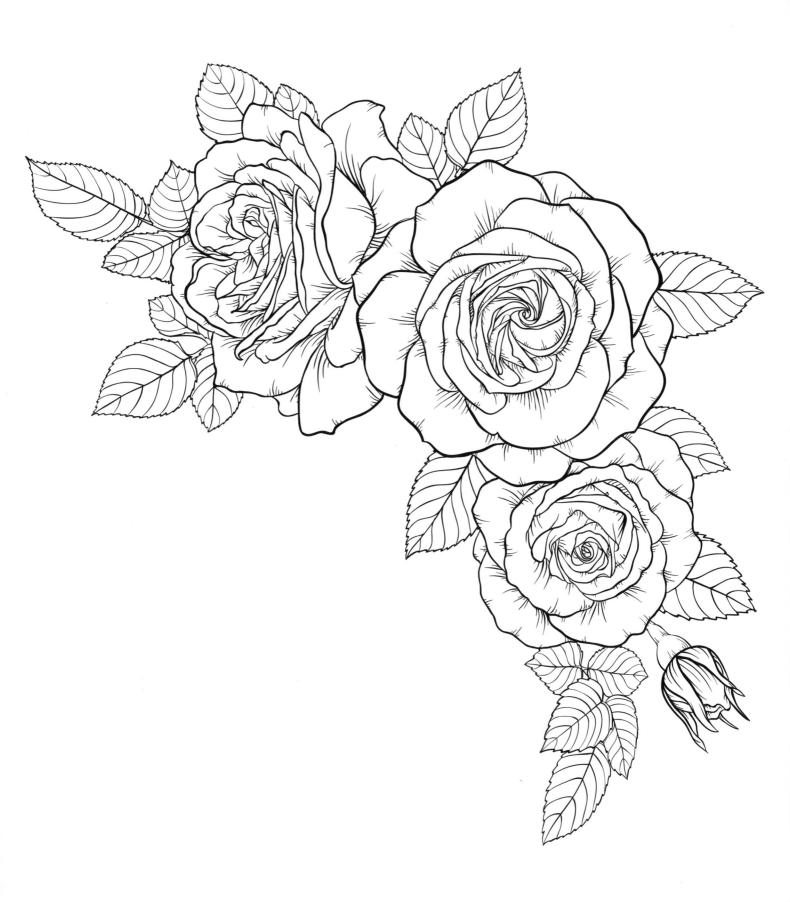

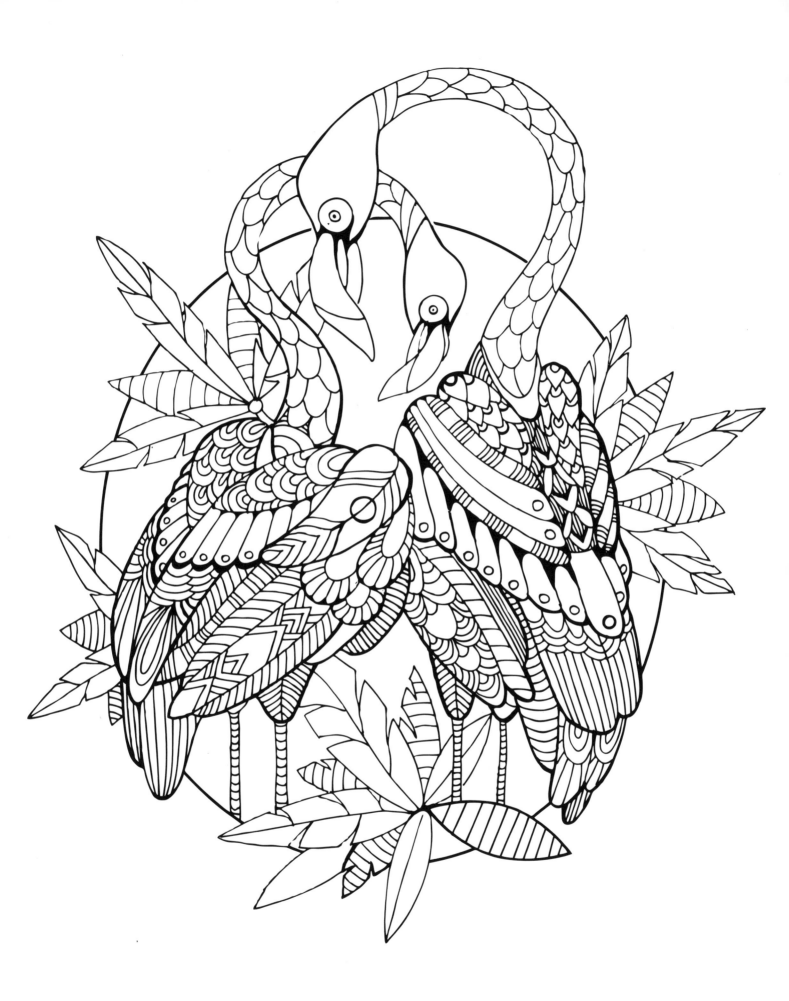

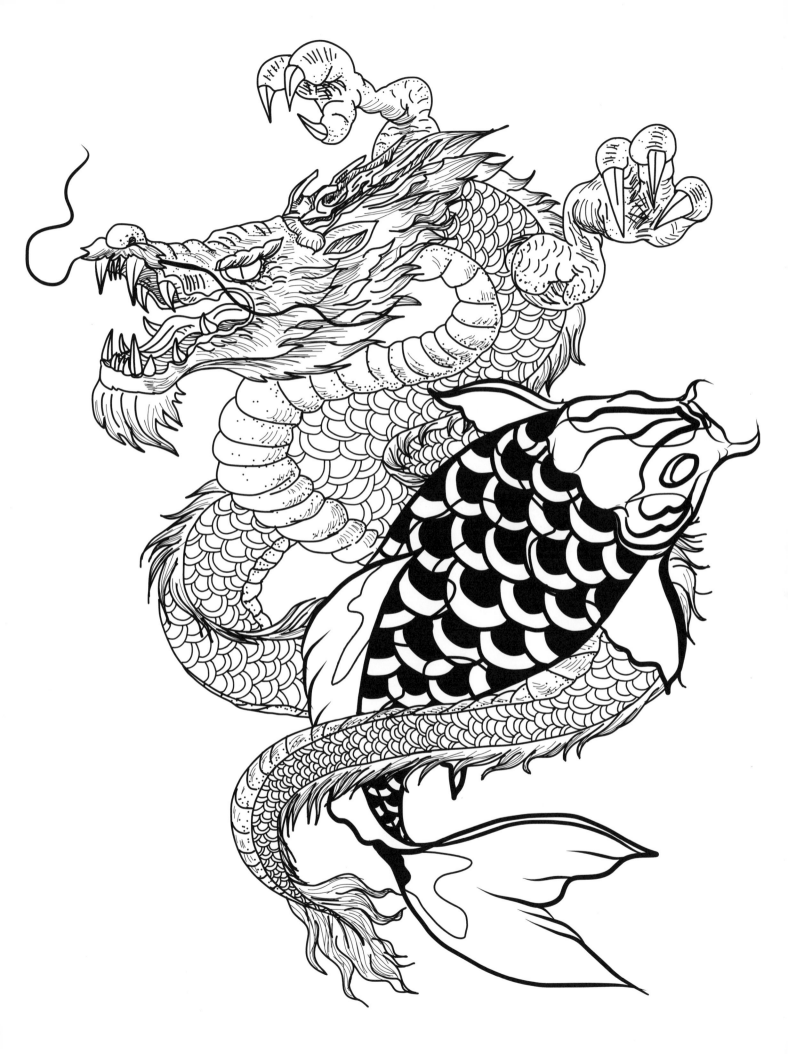

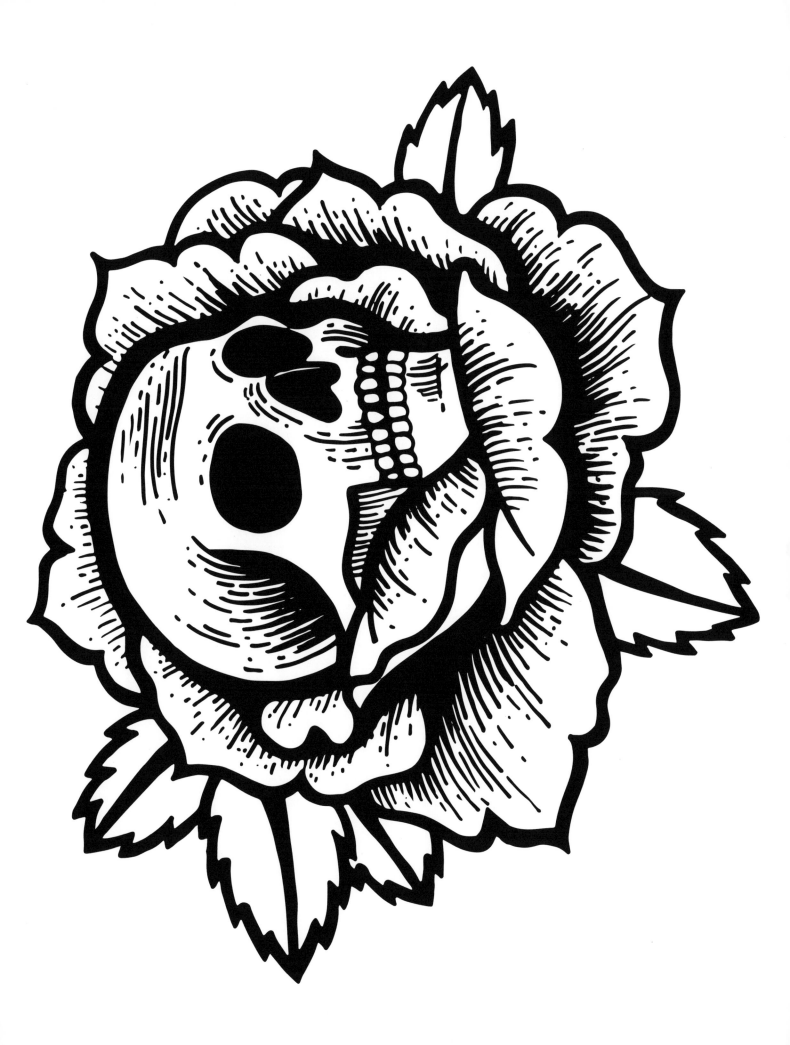

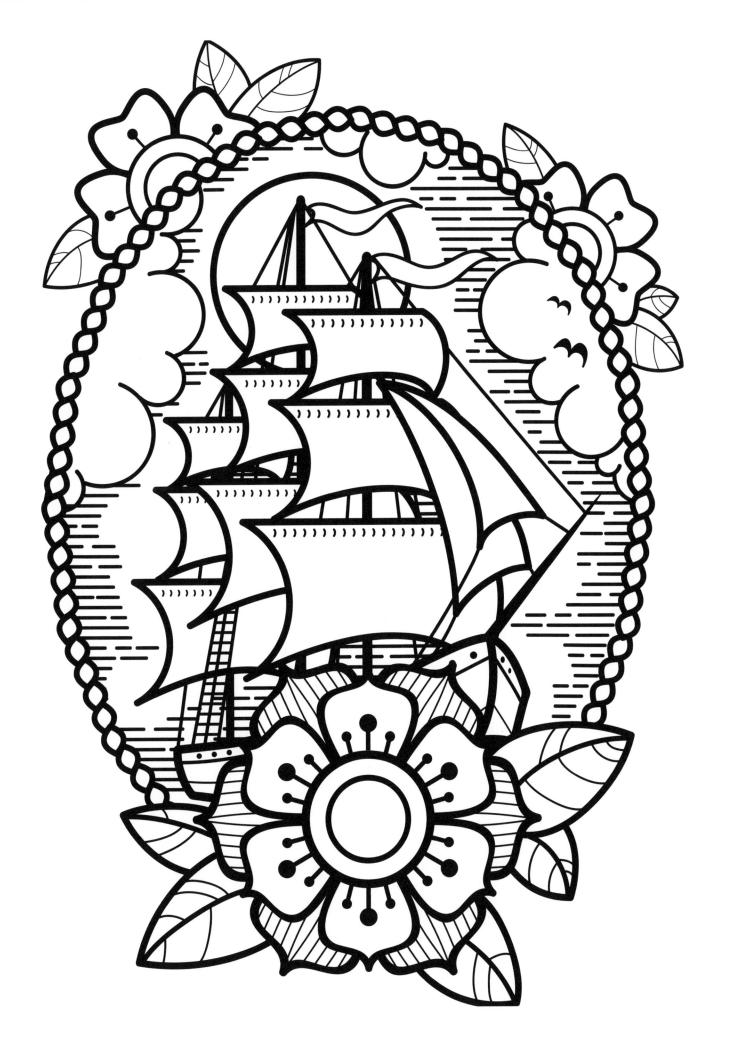